Tina byjan

Praise for *Zen and the Art of Falling in Love*:

'Insightful, clear, humorous, delightful . . . Charlotte Kasl
guides us through the exciting and sometimes daunting
territory of finding a loving mate. A must-read for all people
who value honesty, kindness, and compassion in the affairs of
the heart. I recommend it with my whole heart'
Susan Page, author of *If I'm So Wonderful,*
Why Am I Still Single?

'This compassionate, insightful book takes a much
deeper look at love and romance . . . Charlotte Kasl
does a beautiful job weaving Eastern philosophy into
modern day relationships. I'm inspired!'
Janet Luhrs, author of *The Simple Living Guide*

'What a wonderful and unique book! Full of wisdom on how to
find a partner while maintaining your own integrity and
self-esteem . . . Charlotte Kasl is wise, light-hearted, gentle,
practical, and very supportive of the soul's search for a mate.
Her book deserves to be read and reread'
Jennifer Schneider, M.D., author of *Back from Betrayal:*
Recovering From His Affairs

'Charlotte Kasl deserves some kind of award . . . People
who want depth in relating, who want to get beyond the
shallow water and treacherous rapids of "catch/get caught"
dating trips, and who wish to actually use their relationships
as part of their path of personal and spiritual growth
will find much here to aid that effort'
Rowan Conrad, Ph.D., therapist, Buddhist meditation teacher,
and student of Thich Nhat Hanh's Order of Interbeing

'In this personal exploration of love, relationships, and
spirituality, Charlotte Kasl describes the search for love as a
process that is inseparable from one's personal and spiritual
evolution. This book is a healing guide to this painful,
exasperating, and wondrous and enlightening struggle
to love ourselves and others'
Keith Walker, Buddhist practitioner

www.booksattransworld.co.uk

Also by Charlotte Kasl

IF THE BUDDHA MARRIED: CREATING ENDURING
RELATIONSHIPS ON A SPIRITUAL PATH

A HOME FOR THE HEART: CREATING INTIMACY AND
COMMUNITY WITH LOVED ONES, NEIGHBORS, AND FRIENDS

FINDING JOY: 101 WAYS TO FREE YOUR SPIRIT
AND DANCE WITH LIFE

YES, YOU CAN! A GUIDE TO EMPOWERMENT GROUPS

MANY ROADS, ONE JOURNEY: MOVING BEYOND
THE TWELVE STEPS

WOMEN, SEX, AND ADDICTION: A SEARCH FOR
LOVE AND POWER

ZEN AND THE ART OF FALLING IN LOVE

A Handbook for Finding Love on a Spiritual Path

Charlotte Kasl, Ph.D.

BANTAM BOOKS
LONDON · NEW YORK · TORONTO · SYDNEY · AUCKLAND

ZEN AND THE ART OF FALLING IN LOVE
A BANTAM BOOK : 0 553 81496 6

Originally published in the USA by Arkana,
a division of the Penguin Group, as *If the Buddha Dated*.
First publication in Great Britain

PRINTING HISTORY
Bantam edition published 2003

1 3 5 7 9 10 8 6 4 2

To all people seeking love on a spiritual path

and to
Alissa, Danielle, Alex, Emily, and Mary

Heartfelt thanks

. . . to all the people who helped with this book. Special thanks to my editor, Janet Goldstein, for enthusiasm, wonderful input, and support; to Edite Kroll, my steadfast agent, for help, humor, and friendship; thanks also to Susan Hans O'Connor and Nancy Peske for editing and to Erica Soon Olson for editing and writing instruction.

A bouquet of roses to Rowan Conrad, therapist and senior student of Zen Buddhist teacher Thich Nhat Hanh, for a careful reading and invaluable detailed suggestions for the manuscript. And for input, comments, interviews, friendship, inspiration, humor, and moral support, not necessarily in that order, thank you friends and colleagues: Keith Walker, Stephen Wolinsky, Jane Yank, Jennifer Schneider, Mary Greenfield, Shahir, Qahira, Star, Darvesha, Altazar Player, David Long, Barbara Brady, Jim McNaughton, Alissa Davis, Danielle Davis, Joanna Lester, Jeanine Walker, Dodi Moquin, Debbie Batterson, Johna Koontz, Michelle Moeller, David Marsolek, Michael Sullivan, and Linda Lightfoot.

Contents

Part 2
AWAKEN YOUR DESIRE:
who are you? what do you want?

Part 3
ENTER THE SACRED FIRE:
the journey toward intimacy

Part 4
KEEP LOYAL TO YOUR JOURNEY:
stay awake, stay aware

Part 5
GOING DEEPER:
create a durable fire

Part 6
LIVING IN THE HEART OF THE BELOVED:
we are one with each other

Introduction

What This Book Can and Can't Do For You

This book is about creating love in your life. It begins with bringing awareness, compassion, and loving kindness to yourself, including the parts you tend to disown or want to keep hidden. This journey of self-knowledge may be uncomfortable, sometimes challenging, but it will help you make friends with all of who you are, so you will be free to welcome another person into your heart. I have been on this journey for a long time, and have felt both the freedom of transforming old patterns and the humbling experience of meeting parts of myself that still need compassion and understanding.

You will find that remaining on the spiritual path as you seek a lover or partner involves a journey that affects all of your life – not just the dating, love, romance, and marriage part. You will begin to recognize long-held beliefs that have been shaping much of your behavior, and you will move beyond them with a new awareness that frees you from the past and allows you to see others clearly, so you can create a spiritual union that you can trust.

As you follow this path, you will find that compassion and acceptance replace fear, negative judgment, and worry. You will approach dating with curiosity, fascination, and a light heart, wanting only what is good for yourself and another person. Instead of choosing a partner based on images, pretense, and roles, you will be able to join your journey with another and learn what it means to create a spiritual bond that is flexible and expansive for both of you.

This is a book for men and women of any age or faith, who seek a vibrant human relationship based on authenticity, equality, spirituality, and joy. While it is centered on Buddhist wisdom, I also draw from Christian, Sufi, and other Eastern teachings. Buddhism is more a philosophy for living rather than a religion or dogma – it's about being awake, free from illusions and fear, so that compassion and loving kindness permeate all our relationships. We can all find our Buddha nature – the luminous essence within us – no matter what our belief system.

While this book is a guide to dating on the spiritual path, it is also practical – full of exercises and suggestions designed to help you on your way. In Buddhism, as in Sufism and other spiritual practices, the practical ways we live are not separate from the spiritual path. It is our ability to be present to the moment, yet unattached to the outcome of any situation, that helps help us create intimate relationships.

This book is also playful. If you think about it, dating can be funny, or at least a good melodrama. These teachings will help you relax and watch yourself with bemused compassion when you feel lost or get caught up making painful demands: *I want a lover/a husband/a wife now!* A light heart and sense of humor help us undercut such demands and keep our sense of perspective. From a cosmic point of view, which includes the breadth of our whole life, our romantic turmoil matters very little. It's a passing show, a moment in time.

Speaking of romantic turmoil, this book *doesn't* promise the quick fix or the perfect relationship that so many dating books guarantee. I have no pat formulas that will bring you a 'marriage made in heaven,' get you to the altar, or put the words 'I do' in someone's mouth. Think about all the books out there with surefire ways to lose twenty pounds. They may work in the short term, but to keep the pounds off, you need to make permanent changes not only in your eating and exercise habits, but in your ability to know and love yourself. Everyone knows what a challenge that is. How much more of a challenge, then, to change our lifelong beliefs and habits about relationships, romance, and love.

But if you read this book, and take it to heart, you *can* let yourself be more open and natural so that you know better who you are and what you want. You *can* begin to relax, smile at your fears, and develop the courage to be more authentic and honest. This will allow you to be seen and loved for who you are instead of hiding out and pushing people away. As you feel more secure, you will worry less about how others respond to you and you will find greater intimacy in all your relationships. The desperation to have a partner will give way

15

to learning to live from your essence, which is pure love, compassion, and understanding. At the same time, if you want a lover or a mate, this book will help you find one. Now it's time to begin the journey . . .

Zen and the Art of Falling in Love

Part 1

PREPARATION FOR LOVE:
walking a path of truth
and loving kindness

1

If the Buddha Dated – or anyone on a spiritual path

Of course, the Buddha didn't date. No one really dated in his time. In that culture, as in many others, it would have been considered barbarian to have young men and women chase after each other, left completely on their own to find mates.

The Buddha wasn't a Buddhist either. That term came from his followers. It means the enlightened one, or one who is awake. According to Walpola Rahula's *What the Buddha Taught*, his name was Siddhartha Gautama, son of Queen Maya and Suddhodana, the ruler of the kingdom of the Sakyas. He was married at age sixteen to a beautiful princess, and while the palace provided every comfort imaginable, he wanted to find a solution to the universal suffering of human kind.

At age twenty-nine, shortly after the birth of his first son, he left the palace to become an ascetic, which meant living with extreme simplicity, poverty, and chastity. For six years he wandered about, meeting famous religious teachers, studying their methods and submitting himself to rigorous spiritual practices. But they did not give him the answers he sought, so he abandoned these traditional approaches and, at age thirty-five, became enlightened after sitting for forty-nine days under the Bodhi or Bo tree – the Tree of Wisdom. He saw that there is only one reality – that form is emptiness and emptiness is form – that we are all made of the same substance, all interconnected. For the next forty-five years he taught anyone who sought his wisdom – kings and peasants alike. Rather than saying, 'Worship me,' he taught people to become free of their illusions so they could be in touch with their inner radiance, or, as some say, the luminous essence at the center of their being – the natural wellspring of compassion, kindness, and tranquility. He believed that from this place we would see each other clearly, free of expectations and images from the past.

Siddhartha Gautama became known as Buddha – the enlightened one – but never claimed to be other than a human being. While Buddhism is often portrayed as austere, in reality it embraces all we are as humans. At the same time, it takes us beyond a kind of self-centered narcissism because instead of identifying with the content of our experience, we identify with awareness itself.

Enlightenment is not about becoming divine. Instead it's about becoming more fully human . . . It is the end of ignorance.
—LAMA SURYA DAS, *Awakening the Buddha Within*

Early practitioners of Buddhism were often monastic, committed to poverty and celibacy. That's why there is little discussion of sexuality and relationships in Buddhist writings, along with the fact that many of the teachers are themselves celibate. In the West, however, Buddhist practitioners are beginning to explore how we can attune sexuality and relationships with the spiritual journey.

What would it mean to bring a Buddha consciousness to dating? Instead of feeling a sense of urgency, we would be fascinated by the process of meeting and getting to know new people. Compassion, care, and kindness for others would supersede 'getting someone to be with us.' And we would never try to control another person. We wouldn't put others on a pedestal, nor would we set them below us. We'd remember that on the spiritual path, the purpose of any relationship is to wake up and get to know ourselves and our lover, thoroughly, without judgment or pride. On the spiritual path, we enter into a shared union where we cherish and give to each other, expanding our ability to love unconditionally. We would also accept that the process can be awkward, unpredictable, challenging, and surprising.

In Buddhism there are teachings and practices, but no rigid dogma. You are encouraged to do whatever helps you become more awake. If we dated with a Buddhist consciousness there would be no separate 'rules' for men and women, because seekers on the path are not distinguished by gender. That doesn't mean there aren't male/female differences, it means that instead of automatically categorizing people, we ask again and again, 'Who are you?' We get to know people as individuals

23

without imposing stereotypes on them. In Chapter 9, we'll further discuss the idea of spiritual equality.

Buddhism is about self-knowledge, a fearless exploration of all we are, so we can be friends with ourselves. Dating with a Buddhist consciousness means a willingness to confront anything inside that kindles fear or anxiety. When we start wanting to run away, be deceptive, tell lies, or put on a mask, we need to walk right into our fears, sit down, and talk to them until they become our friends. This doesn't mean we have a goal of getting rid of fear; rather, we accept it as part of our unfolding journey.

We begin our journey always remembering that there is a circular relationship between our ability to know and love another and our ability to know and love ourselves. I hasten to add that loving oneself doesn't mean that we are perfect, fixed, all together, or any of those other common phrases. It means we are fully alive to our humanness – accepting, compassionate, amused.

Ultimately, as we become friends with ourselves and give up demanding that the universe provide us with a lover, we become truly open to meeting a special person with whom to share this journey of awakening.

Suppose you scrub your ethical skin until it shines,
but inside there is no music, then what?

Mohammed's son pores over words,
and points out this and that,

but if his chest is not soaked dark with love,
then what?

24

The Yogi comes along in his famous orange,
but if inside he is colorless, then what?
                                    —KABIR, *The Kabir Book*

2

Ground Yourself With Spiritual Wisdom

I am a passionate seeker after truth which is but another name for God.

—GANDHI

We become spiritually grounded when we make this commitment to ourselves: *More than anything else, I want myself. I want to live with integrity and truth. I'm not going to hide the jewel of who I am, nor will I mask my imperfections. No bargains, no avoiding reality, no conning myself, no lies.* The more we commit to knowing and accepting ourselves, the more we are able to surrender to loving another person because we have nothing to hide and nothing to feel ashamed of. Our spiritual commitment to truth and integrity creates a safe harbor within us – a mooring, a home to return to when the journey gets rough. This is immensely important in the dating process because new love can resurrect our most primitive feelings of fear, hope, dependency, and emptiness. If we know how to soothe our pain and relax into our emptiness, we won't be afraid to be open and honest, regardless of the outcome.

If we succumb to fear, we start holding back, and do that all-too-common dance of getting close, then pulling away. When we remember that our safe harbor depends on our awareness and honesty, we're less likely to make internal compromises, put on masks, or act like a chameleon to attract a partner or keep a hurtful relationship together. If we live by truth we may have pain, but we will always rest securely within ourselves.

Spiritual wisdom transcends all religions and spiritual practices. I've often heard that one should pick a specific path and stick to it. I am a member of The Society of Friends, known as Quakers, I have been initiated as a Mureed – a student of the Sufi path – I practice yoga regularly, attend workshops on quantum psychology, and follow many Buddhist teachings, including the practice of Tonglin. I am also trained as a Reiki master healer. That's my one path. You might ask, how could I call it *one* path?

Awareness is awareness, love is love, compassion is compassion, goodness is goodness. The first precept of the Buddhist order founded by Thich Nhat Hanh is, 'Do not be idolatrous about or bound to any doctrine, theory, or ideology, even Buddhist ones.' The source of truth and wisdom is immaterial. There are no rules, no boxes to fit in, no one way, no absolutes when it comes to grounding yourself in spiritual wisdom. That's why I find no conflict in my affiliation with these different spiritual practices. All of them focus on our moment to moment experience of bringing acceptance, mindfulness, compassion, truth, and love to every aspect of our lives. Said another way, they are about how you live, not what you say you believe.

Because this book draws primarily from these traditions, I'll tell you a little about each one so you can draw on their wisdom. Each tradition has various branches among its followers. These descriptions might help you think about the spiritual wisdom you already have that provides a quiet resting place for your heart and mind.

Buddhism centers around compassion, kindness, truth, awareness, and clear perception of reality. Many regard it more as a philosophy than a religion. Central to the teachings are the four noble truths: First, that suffering is inherent in life. Second, that we create our suffering through our attachments and demands that things be different than they are. We can be attached to money, property, food, belief systems, or other people. In other words, when our minds are busy with scripts, images, and fantasies of what we think we must have, we end up frustrated, disappointed, and unable to live in the moment and appreciate the *what is* of life. We suffer. The third noble truth suggests that we ease our suffering when we cease our endless demands and accept the *what is* of life. The fourth truth is that with complete acceptance of *what is*, and with seeing through all these superficial desires to the essence of all that is, we will live with peace and love.

We can make an important distinction between pain and suffering. While *painful* situations are inherent in life – loss, death, hurt, illness – if we accept them as part of life, we do not suffer so much. To a large degree, suffering results from the turmoil we create when we *demand* that that life be 'fair' and not include obstacles, challenges, or illness. Once we accept these aspects of life, we can more easily cope with them or seek solutions.

Another central aspect of Buddhism is reflected in the eight signposts of being on the spiritual path – Right Aspiration, Right Understanding, Right Speech, Right Action, Right Livelihood, Right Effort, Right Concentration, and Right Mindfulness. As you can see, Buddhism is a very earth-bound approach to living that focuses on our moment-to-moment awareness of every aspect of our life.

Becoming mindful of our attachments or demands in relationships – *you should give me this/do this/be a certain way* – gives us a starting place for loosening the grip of our demanding ego. Whenever we are frustrated, irritated, manipulative, or demanding, we are *attached* to someone or something being different. When we try to mold someone into an image of what we want rather than getting to know and appreciate them as they are, we create separateness, frustration, and loneliness. As we become mindful of our demands and less insistent on having things our way, we feel increasingly peaceful and in touch with our compassion and tenderness.

Buddhists do not refer to God, rather to the essence or energy at the core of all people and all creation. There's no supreme being to lean on or tell you what to do. This can seem frightening at first. But it gives you the ultimate responsibility for your behavior. Buddha taught people to take refuge in themselves, in the truth and in their spiritual community (sangha). Shortly before he died, Ananda, a beloved follower, asked Buddha to leave instructions on teaching the Order of the Sangha. Buddha saw that Ananda was sad and depressed about his imminent death and, in his heartfelt desire to give him and his other students consolation and confidence, he said,

> Surely, Ananda, if there is anyone who thinks that he will lead the Sangha, and that the Sangha should depend on him, let him set down his instructions . . . Therefore, Ananda, dwell making yourselves your island [support], making yourselves, not anyone else, your refuge; making the Dharma [truth/teachings] your island, the Dharma your refuge . . .
> —WALPOLA RAHULA, *What the Buddha Taught*

The Buddha taught that we can find refuge within ourselves through mindfulness of thoughts, body sensations, and attachments. This is not to be confused with being self-centered; rather, it means self-knowing, which takes the shape of knowing and loving all. This frees us to connect with our true essence. One of the key aspects of Buddhism that is crucial to relationships is noticing our attachments or demands that situations or people be different from what they are. Too often, we try to mold people into what we want them to be rather than honoring them as they are.

Another aspect of Buddhism that can help us walk the spiritual path of relationships is the concept of impermanence. Things are always changing – our thoughts, cells, hormones, hairline, consciousness, relationships, and the landscape around us. Instead of trying to freeze the present moment and hang onto it, we need to remember that life is a process of constantly letting go. The ego wants dependable rituals and people who stay the same. But to be free means that we enjoy this touch, this kiss, this sunrise, and then let it go. This is sometimes described as not letting the ground under your feet get too solid, not grasping for security or predictability.

Another aspect of Buddhism is developing a fearless, unbounded compassion for our own suffering and that of others. As you will see in this book, a repeated theme is making peace with all of who you are because it's all sacred, all part of your Buddha nature – your fear, your sadness, your anger, your confusion, your beauty. As we get to know and accept these parts of ourselves, they no longer have power over us. They are just the *what is* of life.

And, of course, one of the central practices in Buddhism is meditation to help us see our own inner process clearly and stop identifying with the endless thoughts that parade through our minds. Central to all Eastern traditions is realizing that we are not our minds, our thoughts, our looks, or our personalities. We are essence, spirit, or energy. Later, in Chapter 31, I will explain the Tonglin meditation practice that provides a powerful way to loosen our attachment to our thoughts and create more spaciousness in our minds and bodies.

*Sufism can be defined as the path of love or opening the heart.** While the heart of Buddhism is coming to realize

*This description of Sufism includes material from conversations with Shahir, Darvesha, and Qahira, all Sufi teachers.

you are part of all that is, Sufism focuses more on emerging as all of who you are. Yet one does not deny the significance of the other. It's more a matter of emphasis. Sufism is Middle East in origin and thus more individualistic than Buddhism, which comes from the Far East where the focus is on the collective rather than the individual. Although Sufism comes from the Moslem tradition, many Sufis in the West do not identify themselves as connected to Islam. By its very nature, Sufism encompasses the spirit that came down through all the prophets and all religions. Just as finding one's Buddha nature does not conflict with other religions, one can take part in Sufi practices in conjunction with other religious traditions.

Sufism is about connecting with the intuitive parts of ourselves so we can attune to the highest vibration in the universe, which is pure love. It's about joining together in the mystical heart. Sufis refer to one God which is all of nature and all sentient life. One of the most sacred phrases in Sufism is 'Iskh Allah Mabud Lillah' – God is love, lover, and beloved. To love each other is to love God and to love God is to love each other – there is no separation. Another phrase is 'La illa ha il Allah' – there is no reality but the one, or but God. This concept is also at the heart of Buddhism.

Music and movement have always been part of Sufi practice, along with numerous breathing exercises and meditations. The Dances of Universal Peace originated in Sufi practice. The Zikr, a chant central to Sufi practice, is based on the words La illa ha il Allah, and when done as a group practice is designed to help bring alive the experience that we are all one sound, one vibration of energy. Ultimately, the Zikr is practiced to dissolve the ego and allow us to feel the tranquility, peacefulness, and safety of The One.

The relationship of teacher to student is one of mutual attunement, friendship, and love. The teacher attunes to what the student is needing at the moment. For example, one time when Shahir, my teacher, was showing me breathing practices, she stopped suddenly and asked, 'How are you doing with the loss of your friend?' I just about burst into tears because that was what I really needed to talk about. Likewise, the student attunes to the teacher and whatever spiritual practices work best. Sufism, like Buddhism, helps people find their inner source of wisdom, which enables them to be truly helpful to others.

Sufism puts a strong emphasis on service to others. The more practices you do, the more capable you become of accepting the responsibility for souls who come knocking on your door in the middle of the night. Attainment of a higher consciousness and an open heart is less a credential than a responsibility. When you start breath work or sound practices, it's like saying 'I am willing to move to a deeper level of service. I am willing to dissolve the false ego that creates the illusion that we are separate so I can do the soul's work.' As you are able to hear the spirit within in you – your connection to the One – you will know just what you need to do.

—QAHIRA, SUFI TEACHER

Sufi gatherings are often festive and colorful with singing, chanting, and various circle dances based on texts from all religious traditions. Women often wear richly printed Indian skirts or wrap scarves around their waists and some of the men wear colorful, non-Western clothing. While many spiritual teachings talk about growing through discipline, austerity, or suffering, Sufism reminds us that spiritual practices to open our hearts can include beauty, joy, and celebration.

Quakers' beliefs are rooted in Christianity although many members and attenders do not consider themselves Christian. Quakers value truth as sacred above all – above books, teachings, rituals, or practices. As with all mystical traditions, Quakerism focuses on the *experience* of love, connection, and spirit as it speaks through us, rather than dogma or symbols.

Quakers talk about 'leadings,' or being 'called' to do something. The commitment to oneself as a Quaker is to listen for this inner guidance and have the courage to follow it. In the Quaker meeting, where Friends sit quietly in a circle, if someone feels moved by spirit to stand up and speak, they do so; otherwise, they remain quiet. (That's a practice nearly all relationships could benefit from.) Traditional Quaker worship is without dogma, icons, ministers, or sacred texts. Everyone is seen as having direct access to spirit or God. There is freedom from all spiritual materialism and an emphasis on service, silence, and simplicity. In this way, Quaker and Buddhist philosophies are the same.

Along with the mystical aspects of their spiritual practices, Quakers have a long history of social activism, believing that we ground our faith by taking action against oppression and injustice and being of service to people who are suffering. The often quoted phrase 'Speak truth to power' serves as a strong reminder of our responsibility to speak up against injustice or oppression, even if we are the lone voice in the crowd.

Quaker meetings have a special committee, sometimes called Ministry and Counsel, whose task is to stay attuned to the spiritual life of the meeting and help it grow and flourish. It's kind of like the Sufi teacher staying attuned to her student. All gatherings, including business meetings, weddings, and memorial services, are referred to as a meeting for worship, which implies that we bring thoughtfulness and reverence to all that we do. One form of caring for each other is through clearness committees. Members can request a committee to help them become clear about a decision, job, relationship, or spiritual concern. Quakers use the concept of feeling clear inside as a touchstone for knowing when you've found the truth about a given situation.

Quakers have a saying: 'Walk cheerfully over the earth seeing [or answering] that of God in everyone.' Buddhists teach us to see the luminous essence in everyone. Sufis talk about all people living in the mystical heart of God. Different words, one message. However you hear it, remember that stillness, practice, and the willingness to reflect inwardly and stop identifying with the rising and falling of your thoughts will all ground you on the spiritual path. As you deepen your commitment to know yourself and make friends with all of who you are, mercy and compassion will emerge naturally as you begin to live from your essence. This, in turn, will free you to give and receive love.

Whatever practices you utilize, ultimately it is your

dedication that will make a difference. You can intone a chant or prayer absentmindedly, dissociate when you meditate, or spout teachings to impress people. Or you can meet each moment of your life with awareness and compassion.

Pema Chodron writes in *Start Where You Are*,

What you do for yourself – any gesture of kindness, any gesture of gentleness, any gesture of honesty and clear seeing toward yourself – will affect how you experience your world. In fact, it will transform how you experience the world. What you do for yourself, you're doing for others, and what you do for others, you're doing for yourself.

3

What Is This Longing for an Intimate Relationship?

I want this music and this dawn and the warmth of your
cheek against mine.

—RUMI, SUFI POET, from *Like This*

You want a partner. It could be wonderful – to have a refuge, a sparring buddy, a helpmate to join you on the journey. We can wish for a person to walk beside us and we can make a concerted effort to find someone without falling off our path. This requires having the spiritual desire to connect, crack our boundaries, and feel love as the spirit of the universe flowing between us.

I have a thirsty fish in me
that can never find enough
of what it's thirsty for!
Let my house be drowned in the wave
that rose last night out of the courtyard
hidden in the center of my chest.

—RUMI, from *Like This*

The Sufi poet Rumi interlaces our desire for human love with our thirst for the divine. The rich images of having a thirsty fish inside, or being drowned in the wave, can be seen as surrender to a lover *and* surrender to bliss. They become one in the same. When we let go completely of our ego and our demands, even for a moment, we taste the sweetness of love. The phrase 'The fish in the water's not thirsty' from the Dances of Universal Peace suggests that we are all thirsty for that which surrounds us, and we only need to open ourselves to the unbounded love that's available to us when our hearts are free.

Our longing for connection is natural to human existence. We are all tribal people and our health, joy, and happiness are intricately tied to interconnecting with others and with spirit. Longing for a lover is an expression of longing to awaken our hearts, to know love.

Sometimes, though, our longing for a lover becomes an attachment that causes suffering. Most popular music is laden with familiar themes of desperation: 'I fall to pieces, each time I hear your name,' 'You're my everything,' 'I can't go on without you.' Most of us who have lost a lover have felt that great big ache inside as we faced our emptiness. We had invested our special friend with the power to give and take away our happiness and suffered as a result because we forgot that spirit is within us and around us. No one can 'make us happy.' If you accept that your longing for a lover is your desire to crack through your rigid ego and be free, you will commit to staying aware on your journey.

Show me the way to the Ocean!
Break these half measures,
these small containers
                              —RUMI, from *Like This*

As an intrepid traveler on the path to love, you open
yourself to whatever comes your way – hurt, fear, neediness, joy, bliss – invite it in, observe it, make friends
with it, and let it pass. This commitment to staying
awake will free you from holding back and allow you to
feel the roar, purr, glow, and breath of spirit rippling
through you, sensuous and alive.

If you seek only refuge, security, and comfort, you
imprison your relationship and the vitality will wane.
Krishnamurti, the renowned spiritual teacher and
author of numerous books, wrote, 'If in a relationship
there is no tension [meaning no deepening of knowledge of self and others], it ceases to be a relationship
and merely becomes a comfortable sleep state, an opiate
– which most people want and prefer.'

Our longing is also our desire to be known completely. Imagine having your beloved look tenderly into
your eyes, knowing all your secrets, having seen you be
crabby and sweet, selfish and generous, and still truly
loving you. Imagine being able to do the same. That is
the potential of a conscious relationship.

Our ego may fight this exploration because it wants
to hold onto cherished beliefs about who we are, what
is right, and what we need. We move toward love
and suddenly our ego throws up a wall. *Danger, back off.*
The ego fears surrender. Our soul, however, longs for us
to crack our shells, leap in the ocean, and become

naked to ourselves and others. In doing so we become free to experience *all that is* within us: the power of our sexuality and passion, creativity, generosity, and tenderness along with the parts of us that are whiny, afraid, dependent, controlling, empty, violent, or needy – not to mention the parts of us that may sink to new depths of sneakiness and manipulation.

While our minds want to categorize these traits as good and bad, they are neither – they simply reflect aspects of our humanness. In Buddhism, there is no judgment of where you are on the path. The joys and the obstacles reflect your momentary state of consciousness. When you get upset, afraid, or obsessed, it's not bad, it's a message. Sometimes it's a scream from within saying *notice me, stop hiding from me, I need your attention.* Become fascinated by and curious about your inner world, bring minute-to-minute awareness of your judgments, reactions, fears, and hurts, without shame or saying, 'I shouldn't feel that way.' How you feel is how you feel, what you think is what you think. Instead of stopping the flow of these thoughts and feelings, be with them, observe them, explore their origins. They are your teachers. All transformation starts with awareness.

4

Stay Loyal to Your Journey

Your daily life is your temple and your religion. Whenever you enter into it take with you your all.
—Kahlil Gibran, *The Prophet*

You are unique in all the world. You have gifts, talents, strengths, and a capacity for a wide range of emotions. Just as we have spring, summer, fall, and winter, just as the oceans rise and fall, just as the moon waxes and wanes, you have an inner world that is fluid and shifting. You have a rich potential to feel love and hate, joy and sadness, tenderness and passion. Your journey is to know yourself.

Staying loyal to your journey means you never abandon yourself by compromising your integrity or discounting your intuition or the signals that come from your body – the knot in the gut, emotional detachment, or loss of energy that signals something is amiss. You learn to realize when you 'hit your edges' – when you feel backed up against a wall, scared to see what you see, know what you know, or feel what you feel. When

41

people hit an edge they usually run away by going numb, distracting themselves, changing the subject, counter-attacking, overindulging in food or drink, or blaming.

We may hit an edge when someone hurts us, or when someone loves us more than we love ourself. It is harder for many people to allow love to pierce their heart than to have chaotic, painful relationships. I remember that when I was an adolescent a very dear young man named Eddie pursued me. I liked him, I enjoyed being with him and, one day, I just froze up and couldn't talk to him. Many years later I came to understand that I feared his love would penetrate my heart and open up a torrent of buried heartaches and pain. It was less threatening to date people who emotionally starved me.

To be loyal to your journey is to care for yourself and remember that at your center, you are a luminous essence capable of compassion and love. Buddhists use many images to describe our inner perfection: the sun behind the clouds, a pot of gold underneath the ground, a jewel that is buried in mud beside the road. Using the jewel image, we can remember that the precious stone is beautiful, radiant, and shining, but unless someone digs it up and washes off the mud, it cannot shine or be appreciated. Most of us have coverings over the jewel that is within us – the false beliefs and masks that block our connection to our perfect essence.

According to Stephen Wolinsky in *The Tao of Chaos*, we all start life as an *essential* being – completely spontaneous and free, without memories or associations. He writes, 'As we are conditioned, programmed, and taught how to look, how to be, how to behave, how to act, how to imagine, how to feel and how to think, our essence becomes submerged between all the "I-dentities" we take on.' We learn to please Mom, smile for company, get good grades and make endless adaptations to be noticed and loved. Eventually we lose contact with our essence and even come to fear it. According to Wolinsky, 'An I-dentity, if it enters this emptiness . . . imagines annihilation, nonexistence, or death. This inner emptiness is the inner Essence which we all seek and which contains essential qualities like love, peace, power, invulnerability, and so on, and which is intrinsic to the nature of Essence.'

A question Stephen Wolinsky posed at a workshop to help people feel their essence was this: 'Without mind, memory, or associations, what is love?' I drew a complete blank in response to his question, because without mind, memory, or associations, there is only essence.

Staying loyal to your journey means learning to recognize the adaptations and 'I-dentities' we have adopted to survive and please others. We need to first acknowledge them and realize they are only the coverings over our essential being. They are the voices that say *Be careful, don't get too close, you can't trust anyone, who needs love anyhow?* They are the ways we protected ourselves as children. But we are no longer children. We can now see beyond our childhood perceptions of safety. As we loosen the grip of these 'I-dentities', and stop believing they are real, we become freer to resonate with the heart of a lover – touching, giving, receiving, connecting.

The spiritual path wrecks the body and afterwards restores it to health. It destroys the house to unearth the treasure, and with that treasure builds it better than before.

—RUMI, from *Like This*

To be loyal to our journey is to know the rhythm, tone, and pulse of our essential inner world – the song that is ours alone. When two people bring the richness of their inner music to each other, they bring the possibility of a new composition, of counterpoint, harmony, voices weaving together, creating a magical composition. If we're disconnected from the music of our essence, and attempt to find happiness through another's song, there will be dependency and a relationship without harmony.

Some questions to explore as you consider forming a relationship on the spiritual path:

- What are the thoughts and beliefs (the false 'I-dentities') that limit your life?
- What are the ways you run away when you hit your edges?
- What will help you stop running away and sit still when you hit your edges?
- What would help you have the courage to look inside, challenge your beliefs, and live with anxiety, confusion, and discomfort?

You might need to ask yourself these questions many times and listen in the quiet to hear the answers. You might also hear the ego being indignant – *How dare you question my thoughts, my personality, my beliefs.* But don't give way.

By wrecking your illusions you can find the jewel that is you. *The spiritual path is a process of unmasking ourselves rather than changing or repairing ourselves.* Our task is to crack through and soften the layers upon layers of personas and masks we have donned to protect us from the false core beliefs that cover our hurts, losses, and loneliness.

We start by being aware of our masks, curious about their purpose, amused by their cleverness, yet always remembering that masks are simply that – they can't love. We can remove these coverings in a thousand ways: When we soften our eyes, and say, 'I care about you.' When we stop showing off and say, 'I'm afraid, I feel incompetent.' We might quietly say to our beloved, 'I'm feeling afraid, can we sit together in this fear?' Most of all we need to recognize our fears as ours, and not attribute them to the weather, the stars, or another person.

When you drop your mask, you invite others to do the same. Some people will accept the invitation, others may run away – because they start to feel acutely aware of their own coverings. They may walk away and you may endure even more loneliness. But remember, if you want love and friendship, if you want to know beauty, you must walk the path undisguised.

Staying loyal to our journey means living with integrity, even when it hurts. If we meet someone and know he or she isn't a good fit, we don't stay with them out of convenience while we wait for someone better to come along. We don't cause harm to ourselves or others by suddenly abandoning our lives as we rush blindly toward an illusion.

We need to be aware of our inner trickster – the ego in its many disguises lulling us to sleep. Our trickster is the con artist within – rationalizing, making excuses, pushing away, dreaming of the perfect prince, thinking no one is good enough, or making us believe we can find someone who will take care of us and allow us to do whatever we want, so we can give up responsibility for ourselves. Sometimes our trickster slips on the mask of a wise one or teacher, full of advice and counsel for others, in order to deflect us from our own insecurities and fears. Remember, the trickster's act is all a covering for fear. It's the wall that keeps us from our essence. On the spiritual path we must become a gentle warrior – curious, kind, and alert to our own con games – whispering to ourselves, *wake up.*

5

Notice the Stories You Tell Yourself

The causes of troubled relationships and fears about dating, or giving oneself to love, are born in the stories we tell ourselves. We experienced a troublesome event, had an emotional response, and then we created a story to explain it or alleviate our pain. Over time, we repeated the story until it took on a life of its own and started to become a script we followed. Laura enjoyed taking violin lessons as a young girl but found them difficult. One day, when she was struggling with a particular piece, her teacher became frustrated and said, 'You just don't have any musical talent.' From then on, Laura shied away from anything to do with music. She wouldn't sing, dance, or play an instrument. The story, 'You have no musical talent,' was so pervasive it became like concrete in her brain. She wouldn't even sing happy birthday at parties and was overwhelmed with anxiety when asked to take part in folk dancing at a school gathering.

Many years later she met a man who loved to dance. He invited her to go with him to a local dance club one night. 'No, I can't dance!' she exclaimed, feeling intense anxiety. 'Hey, I didn't mean to scare you,' he said seeing her panic. 'Who told you you couldn't dance?'

When she recounted the violin story and the belief that she had no talent, he smiled and said, 'But that doesn't make it true.' His remark was like a laser beam of light shattering her rigid belief. Slowly, with his help and patience, she became willing to learn some easy dance steps. When she discovered that not only could she learn to dance, she enjoyed it, she realized she had limited her life drastically because of a story she made up as a result of one harsh, insensitive remark made long ago.

We all make up stories based on how our parents, church, religion, and teachers treated us. These beliefs get hardwired into the limbic system of the brain and we believe them as if they were absolute truths rather than ideas put into our minds. They become the 'knee-jerk' reactions we can't seem to control. We organize our experiences around these false beliefs and they become the filter through which we interpret and react to people and situations. If we have the belief 'I'll always be abandoned,' we create situations where we'll be abandoned, and forget to notice when people are loyal friends. Our task on the spiritual path is to stop repeating the same old stories and become aware of all the ways we keep proving our stories are true.

While we may, as individuals, have many personality traits, according to the Enneagram, which is based on ancient Sufi teachings, there are nine basic personality types and each person has one that predominates, although we usually have some traits of the others. According to Kathleen Hurley, author of *My Best Self*, underlying each personality type is 'an unconscious motivation that causes [us] to respond to life in a way so consistent as to become the driving force shaping [our] lives.' There are many interpretations of the Enneagram and the nine personality types. One I find most useful is Stephen Wolinsky's reference to false core beliefs or false core drivers that underlie the nine personality types. These false core beliefs reflect the conclusions about ourselves we came to as the result of our early childhood traumas or experiences. Wolinsky lists nine basic false core beliefs that correspond to each of the nine personality types described in the Enneagram. Your false core belief has a tremendous effect on how you react to situations and whom you are attracted to for friends and lovers. As we release the false core beliefs, or become less fused with them, we become freer to live from our essence. See if any of the following resonate with you:

1. There must be something wrong with me.
2. I am worthless.
3. I have an inability to do . . .
4. I'm inadequate.
5. I don't exist.
6. I'm alone.
7. I'm incomplete, there is something missing.
8. I am powerless.
9. There is no love – it's a loveless world.

Do any of these false core beliefs feel familiar? Do they suggest why you have been attracted to certain people in your life?

What if we listened for a whole day or a week, or the rest of our lives, to all the stories we tell ourselves, seeing them for what they are – a defense against our false core beliefs which keep us from connecting with our essence, which is free, open, spontaneous, and creative? What if we explored each story, carefully, tenderly, while reminding ourselves we are now adults, able to make choices? Our ego would flare up because it believes our stories are *real*. *There are a lot of jerks out there! She was totally irresponsible! My parents were mean! I* wasn't *taught how to love!*

Our ego may also be indignant if we are lighthearted: *Are you making fun of my pain?* One of our biggest stories is that our pain is serious. From a Buddhist perspective, we can remember that pain is seen as an inevitable aspect of human existence. It's our attachment to being free of pain that creates suffering. Yes, we sometimes hurt, and it certainly matters. Yes, past events affected us and yes, we've had to face tough things in life, but the trauma is over now. We free ourselves by bringing awareness to the moment and experiencing life in the present, unbounded by memories from the past.

So, when you think of running an ad in the personals, having a first date, feeling sexual attraction, or being loved, first notice the stories that come to mind. Notice the sensations in your body or any changes in your energy level. When I get invested in my negative stories, I feel a dry, flat sensation in my chest. Remember: our stories are locked into place by fear –

fear of experiencing the current moment, the emptiness beneath all the chaos and activity created by our stories, and fear of experiencing a loving connection that pierces our heart and reveals both our grief and joy. If you can loosen the grip of these false beliefs even a little bit, your life will have more flow.

One helpful technique common to Buddhist practice is that when we get absorbed with our thinking, we simply say 'thinking' and bring our attention to our breath as it goes in and out. The idea is to create openness and spaciousness by being less identified with our thoughts.

Underneath our stories we often find painful memories. Meditation, counseling that uses EMDR (eye movement, desensitization, and reprocessing), and quantum psychology work as described by Stephen Wolinsky are some methods for going beyond false core beliefs. (See references in the Resources.) The key to allowing the memories into our heart is compassion. We can remember that we were hurt or alone, and did the best we could to comfort ourselves. We can say to that part of ourselves, *I understand why you felt that way, but it's over now, we're grown up, we can take care of ourselves.*

6

Accept the Dance of Oneness and Separateness

> *Imagine an infant, some two months old, cradled in his mother's arms, nursing . . . adrift in the oceanic, timeless, boundless world of infancy, his being and that of his caretaking human partner are merged.*
>
> —MAGGIE SCARF, *Intimate Partners*

Intimacy requires an ability to both merge and be separate, to come together and be apart, like oscillating on a giant swing from oneness to separateness, creating a constant rhythm and, for many, feelings of anxiety. We sometimes feel anxious because falling in love and starting a new relationship resurrects any buried feelings about our original attachment to our mother or a primary caregiver. We were once completely merged with our mother and, often unconsciously, we still desire to find that feeling of union. We want someone to completely enfold us and take care of us.

As children we needed to be held and protected so we wouldn't feel cast into an abyss; at the same time we needed to be free to leave our mother's arms to explore the fascinating world around us. This required a mother who could hold us close one minute, and release us the next. If our parents had unresolved problems with oneness or separateness, they may have been indifferent when they held us or uncomfortable when we wanted to be separate, explore interests, or have friends of our own. Our parents may have written scripts for us or seen us as a reflection of their own worth, rather than as separate people.

From her earliest memory, Margie remembered her mother encouraging her to be a doctor. She gave her doctor toys, books on doctors, and endlessly talked about her daughter's future career.

It was as if she wanted to be able to say, 'My daughter, the doctor.' I don't think she ever asked me what I wanted to be. She also talked about what I ate nearly every day and constantly weighed me – you'd think it was her body. She was incredibly concerned with the status of boys I dated and spent a fortune trying to dress me in very classy feminine clothes when I preferred blue jeans. She was obsessed with me, but never really interested in who I was.

Margie felt gripped by guilt whenever she explored activities she enjoyed that didn't meet with her mother's approval, and felt incredibly disloyal when she dated a man from a lower middle-class background. Her mother missed no opportunity to cut him down. Margie's mother fits the classic picture of a narcissist – someone who sees the world through her own eyes, writes scripts for others, and is unable to understand her impact on the people around her.

Intrusive or narcissistic parents give their children the covert message that forging a separate identity is a crime punishable by abandonment. In other words, the parent instills the message, 'You hurt me if you disagree with me, you hurt me if you love someone else or won't be who I want you to be.' This puts children in a double bind between their natural desire for their authentic self, and their desire for their parents' approval. False beliefs become ingrained: 'I'm responsible for everyone's happiness.' 'The truth hurts people.' 'You are going to hurt me.' 'Being myself is wrong.' This makes both the spiritual path and relationships very difficult because of the tremendous fear of being authentic or bringing up conflict or even having an opinion. Until we become emotionally separate from an intrusive or controlling parent and release the accompanying guilt – which is really a cover for our rage and anger – we are likely to get into distant or chaotic push-pull relationships.

Whenever someone gets close to us we tend to see them as the critical or intrusive parent, and misinterpret their motivation and intent. To talk openly about our fears and opinions feels like pulling fish hooks out of our throat. Instead of experiencing oneness and separateness, we often vacillate between compliance and defiance – being the good child or the bad child, the one who obeys or the one who rebels.

Separating from a controlling parent can feel as if we're being disloyal and cruel. For some, it feels like giving up an addiction. And the guilt – the symptom of withdrawal – can be gut-wrenching.

Releasing guilt requires that we connect with our underlying resentment and anger. This crime of breaking a symbiotic loyalty tie is a necessary one, however, because only through forging a separate identity and finding our authentic voice, can we give birth to our own true self and see others clearly.

Margie was determined to separate from her mother. While moving two thousand miles away to attend college helped, her mother's voice still lived in her head, and she still felt guilty if she didn't call every few days. With intensive counseling she slowly realized she wasn't responsible for her mother's well-being and that she had the right to love another. Two years later she took a major step in separating from her mother by revealing she was in love with a woman. In the week before she mailed her 'coming out' letter she had digestive problems and flashes of anxiety, but mailed the letter anyhow, much to her eventual relief. As the old beliefs became less tenacious, she became freer to deepen her bond with Ellie.

A healthy relationship consists of two people, devoted to each other, being true to their path as well as being intimate with each other. We need to willingly open the door for our beloved to spend time realizing his or her passions and life goals. If we feel threatened when our partner feels enthusiasm for work or hobbies, it's our job to recognize jealousy and possessiveness as *our* problem. *Hmm, I'm getting jealous, even rageful. What's fueling these feelings? What old wounds are these stories 'protecting'?*

If you are the one being pressured to limit yourself or give up your dreams to placate your partner, it's important to withstand the pressure and continue on your path calmly, kindly, and with compassion for your partner's predicament. You can let your partner know you're not withdrawing your love, you are expanding your life. Your beloved may or may not hear you, but staying true to yourself is the only hope for a spiritually centered relationship, and it's the only way to stay on your journey.

In any relationship you can notice your feelings when you come together and leave to be apart. Is the transition smooth, free, and open, or is it sticky, wrenching, fearful? Do you often stay longer than you meant to or linger on the phone because it's painful to separate? Do you pressure your new love to be with you, and feel empty when you're alone? Just notice. Stay with the experience. What is it telling you?

As we evolve on the spiritual path, we find a balance between being together – welcoming, present, and alive – and being separate, because life is rich either way.

Our emotional experience of making transitions between oneness and separateness parallels the ambivalence most people feel on the path of spiritual development. We want inner peace but we're scared to surrender our rigid ego or interrupt our busy schedule to experience stillness (or the agitation that comes when we attempt to be still). We want a partner, but we shy away from pain or discomfort, or the possibility of loss. We want intimacy, but we don't want to give up doing things our way, or to let go of our longing to have someone take care of us. These fears come from the stories that conceal our wounds.

It might help to remember that at an energy level,

win or lose its all the same: our tears of joy and tears of pain are both one energy, the flow of who we are. We can either bargain, hold back, and hang onto comfort and security, or we can take a deep breath, and say *take me*, and leap into the fire.

7

Be Willing to Cook in the Spiritual Fire

Gamble everything for love . . .
Half-heartedness doesn't reach into majesty.
You set out to find God,
but then you keep stopping for long periods
at mean-spirited roadhouses.
Don't wait any longer.
Dive in the ocean,
leave and let the sea be you . . .
                    —RUMI, from *Say I Am You*

While most streams of Buddhism take a contemplative stance on passion, pleasure, and pain, Sufism encourages us to be open to our passions – to dive into the sea, to become at one with the beauty and power of the waves.

New love is a rich time for the spiritual warrior. Not only are we challenged to face our most primitive feelings of longing, hunger, love, loss, and fear, we are challenged to welcome feelings of pure joy, ecstasy, sexual pleasure, and bliss. Many people are afraid of expansive energy washing through their body, cracking the boundaries of their limitations, exposing them to the vastness of all they are. If you allow yourself to feel this energy you will be richly rewarded. You will find a tender spot in your heart that allows you to embrace all human experience and to love. Many people find themselves awash in tears when the covering over their heart slips away. They are touched by a small gesture of kindness, inebriated by the fragrance of lilac blossoms infusing the air on a balmy spring evening.

If we can realize that everything is made of one energy – our hearts, bodies, minds, thoughts, emotions, feelings, hurts – it will be easier to jump into the spiritual fire. Nothing is better or worse than anything else. It's all part of the cosmic energy, the *what is* of life. No matter what we've done, how much we've hurt, how ashamed we feel, it's just energy, just stuff that separates us from our perfect essence.

The false core beliefs we have developed and maintained through our stories puts limits on the free flow of energy in our bodies: be careful, don't get too excited, don't be so loud, so exuberant, so passionate, so wild. My colleague and friend Marylee and I often joke about WASP (white Anglo-Saxon Protestant) damage. Keep a firm upper, a tight lower, don't slurp your soup or suck on an orange, don't indulge yourself in more than one fudge brownie, and for God's sake don't ever let anyone hear you fart. How on earth do we go from this kind of conditioning to becoming an open-hearted lover? Physical lovemaking is messy, juicy, smelly, rowdy, funny – there's always an extra arm. If we are open to the power and humor of lovemaking, it expands our energy from our toes to the roots of our hair.

The spiritual warrior hides from nothing. We jump into the fire, we dive into the ocean. We become the sea. In fact, we are already part of the sea of all creation, it's only an illusion that keeps us apart. To allow ourselves free-flowing energy is to say *Take me. I surrender. I'm open to feeling everything inside.* This does not mean we are without discipline or good judgment. It means we fear nothing that is human and natural.

Surrender actually makes us feel safe, because there is nothing left to hide. When we are open and unafraid, we cease being half-hearted with each other. Our words and eyes freely convey *I delight in your company. I care for you.* We release ourselves from the misery of holding back and playing it safe.

In the process of opening ourselves, old childhood feelings may be laid before us. Suddenly, we feel like a hurt three-year-old. We want to cling. We start worrying, we get scared, forget our responsibilities, and churn with anxiety.

Our growth begins when we realize we are facing parts of ourselves that have always been there. It's not the relationship, it's not the other person. No one made us feel that way, they simply touched a place in us that was not clear. It's not easy. We moan, *Oh, God, I just agreed to see a movie I hate. I just had sex when I didn't want to. I smiled when I was angry. I pressured my new love to stay with me when I knew she wanted to go home.* Don't be afraid. You've thrown a log on the spiritual fire. You've hit an edge, now sit with it, don't run away, don't eat a cookie, don't turn on the TV, don't go shopping. Sit down and simmer. Breathe. Be gentle, make friends with that part of you. Try having a conversation between your scared part and your inner spiritual guide, or your Buddha nature. Go into the story behind the story behind the story.

Remember: you can't accept what you haven't experienced and faced. You can't release what you won't grasp or feel. If you're always trying to make life smooth, you won't meet your dragons. You're big now, you can open the closet door, turn on the light and see the fearsome thing, which is probably a little paper dragon trying to roar to stave off fear.

As we make changes, our ego taunts us: *Don't let him see you so close, he'll know you're defective and bad.* It's the paper dragon again. When the ego wants life in all its little compartments – predictable, neat, secure – smile and answer back, *Oh, little child, let me rock you. I understand you are afraid, it's all right. I'm big, I can protect you.*

We sometimes tell ourselves the story that because life was easy before we met a lover, our anxiety and agitation is the fault of our new partner. Remember, love brings up anything that's hiding. While life may have been easier before, it may help to remember that the possibilities for spiritual growth speed up immensely when we become vulnerable and engaged with someone. Suddenly the mask isn't slipping away, it's being ripped off. It's time to awaken. Fast.

> *Stay in the Spiritual Fire*
> *Let it cook you*
> *Be a well-baked loaf,*
> *and lord of the table.*
> *You've been a source of pain,*
> *Now you'll be the delight.*

—RUMI, from *Like This*

Don't take Rumi's encouragement to stay in the spiritual fire to mean you should be in a painful relationship that scalds you. The spiritual fire is one of transformation, not third-degree burns. We seek a partner to walk beside us, cherish us, and help us experience unity and oneness. If we press our edges too hard and get thrown off course, it's good to back off and rest. Find your edges, lean on them, nudge yourself, but if you become overwhelmed, take a breath, relax. Remember, it's all a story being played out and you are the author. It's not supposed to be a Greek tragedy!

Being able to take the heat of the spiritual fire takes practice. I've met many people who live an isolated life – reading books, watching TV, or sitting at a computer – yet fantasize about suddenly having a fine relationship. How's it to happen? It's unlikely. We don't suddenly bare our heart to someone when we haven't talked openly in years. We become more natural and relaxed with people through spending time with friends, revealing ourselves, settling conflicts, and taking on adventures. Our path is not so much to find a lover as to be a good lover of life, of all people. There isn't just one magical relationship, there is the honesty we bring to all relationships. How can we tell someone what we want in bed with our clothes off, when we're scared to invite a friend to the movies? It's a process. We can't play a concerto after our first music lesson. We need to practice.

8

Be Guided by Spirit, Not Ego

There are many dating books with numerous rules about the right thing to do and say when dating. *On the spiritual path, the 'rules' are simple. Simply ask yourself, am I being guided by spirit or by my rigid ego?*

Before differentiating between spirit and the rigid ego, I'd like to say a few words about ego. Ego is not an enemy to be broken or demolished, as is often portrayed in spiritual literature. We don't want to get rid of the ego, we want to soften it, make it porous and receptive, so information, thoughts, and compassion flow in and out. A healthy ego allows us to have the strength of our convictions yet be open to others. Psychological literature often refers to ego strength – a sureness about ourselves that rests calmly inside, the will to actualize our dreams, or stand fast to our beliefs without worrying about the consequences.

By contrast, the *rigid or inflated ego* is concrete and dualistic – right-wrong, good-bad, friend-foe. It is tethered to past experiences that have become hardwired in the brain, resulting in rigid beliefs, fear of change, and an inability to see the many sides of a situation. It believes the stories we've made up are reality and doesn't realize that they are only the cover over our essence. The voice of the rigid ego is intense, urgent, worried, afraid. It says *I've got to have someone, I can't stand being alone. There's something wrong with me for not having a lover.* We cling to the first person we meet, afraid there will never be another. Honesty, integrity, and peace of mind give way to grasping, emptiness, and conniving. Our self-worth is outside of us, attached to having a lover.

The rigid ego is fueled by fear of meeting the dreaded false core beliefs — I'm bad, a loser, unlovable, and so on. To deflect this fear, the inflated ego dons a mask and becomes artificial in relationships. If, for example, on a first date we become attached to being asked out a second time, our ego shifts to control mode — we censor our words, second-guess what our date wants to hear, or try to sell ourselves in some way. This leaves us a stranger to ourself and the person we are meeting. In fact, there has been no authentic connection; it's only our personas that have met.

We are also caught in our inflated ego when we lose perspective on our immediate situation. We're like the teenager who 'will die' if he or she can't go to a certain rock concert or see a certain friend. Because we tell ourselves it's absolutely crucial that we are invited out, have sex, have *great* sex, receive flowers, or are remembered on our birthday, we create turmoil and anxiety. It's not being turned down or left alone on a Saturday night that causes pain, it's the meaning we give to these events and our *demand* that such things not happen.

While we can have preferences, the minute we start insisting that people and situations be different, we create internal turmoil – anger, hostility, sadness, and so on. It's our attachments that lead us to donning a mask, blaming others, or feeling incomplete.

There are some ways to distinguish between spirit and ego. The following are examples of getting caught in the ego.

Boasting of our accomplishments to impress someone.

Defending and criticizing ourselves and others.

Hiding our accomplishments and intelligence to protect another's ego.

Hiding our vulnerability – fears, discomfort, questions, care, tenderness.

Lying, being deceitful, seductive, or manipulative, whether overtly, covertly, or by omission.

Talking on and on about ourselves or others and putting on a fake exterior – cheery, cool, tough, charming, sweet, wise one.

Looking to someone as the perfect person, savior, parent.

Being a chameleon by 'reading' people, then telling them whatever they want to hear.

Pressuring someone to be sexual.

Using sex to keep a relationship.

Giving frequent unsolicited advice.

Plotting to change the other person.

Retaliating when we're mad.

Harming ourselves when we feel hurt – with food, drugs, self-abuse . . . and much more. I'm sure you can think of other examples.

Underlying all these behaviors is fear: Fear of being spontaneous and natural and trusting your instincts. Fear of simply sitting with your internal discomfort, anxiety, shame, and emptiness. Fear of not knowing what to do. We feel all of these fears at times, maybe even quite often.

Tuning into our ego-driven behavior requires that we become the clear-seeing witness of our motivation. We go beneath our stories and knee-jerk reactions and ask *What's really going on with me?* Often we're angry and don't want to admit it. Or we're afraid of losing someone, and don't want to feel sad. The key is self-observation and acceptance. *Hmm. I'm really doing a sales pitch on this guy. What am I afraid of?*, or *Hmm. I'm really worried about saying the 'right thing.' What's that about?*, or *I suddenly have an urge to seduce his best friend. Where's that coming from?* Only by slowing down and reflecting on our own processes and motives can we soften our ego. Zen talks about 'becoming the sovereign of our bodies and minds,' and about looking through our ego stories and associated fears so we see ourselves, other people, and situations as they are – undistorted.

Coming at a situation from a different angle, we can ask ourselves *If I didn't give advice, if I didn't boast of my accomplishments, if I didn't seduce his best friend, what would I feel?* Lonely, stupid, sad, invisible, unlovable, or defective? We need to tell ourselves we can handle these feelings. It's better to meet them than to lose our path.

We are wise to resist the powerful temptation to act out of our inflated ego and instead ask ourselves *How can I stay centered in spirit? How can I do no harm to myself or another person?* These are essentially the two aims of Buddhist practice: experiencing the clear mind that sees things as they are and the compassionate heart that embraces all people.

Sometimes when we're feeling hurt, it can help to remind ourselves of a basic truth: *some people will like us and some people won't.* Everyone is seeing each other through the stories they create. You. Me. Everyone. No matter how hard we try, we will fit with some people and not others. So you might as well give up dancing in someone else's shoes, and just be yourself. That way, you'll be less lonely, you'll become a good friend to yourself, and your feet won't hurt.

When we operate from spirit we move in the direction of the following:

We see ourselves, situations, and other people clearly.

We listen intently, becoming attuned to the other's experience and not pasting them into our story lines.

We reveal ourselves in the interest of making an authentic connection, not impressing or placating someone.

We present ourselves as we are without enhancing or diminishing ourselves.

We ask for what we want without demanding it or being upset if we don't get it.

We stay in touch with our inner experience and reactions. We are guided by internal cues and experience.

We speak the truth as best we can — kindly, with compassion — not to change someone, but because truth is our path and the only foundation for loving relationships.

We bring a broad perspective to all events and remember that everything is an experiment in being evermore aware, present, and loving.

We are on safe ground when we blend our desire for a partner with our desire to know ourselves and be fully awake. Ego says *I want someone to fill me up.* Spirit says *I'll have someone to help me wake up, to challenge my blind spots and be a companion and playmate on the journey.*

9

Spiritual Equality:
one set of rules for men and women

Seeds feed awhile on ground,
then lift up into the sun.

So you should taste the filtered light
and work your way toward wisdom
with no personal covering.

That's how you came here, like a star
without a name.

—RUMI, from *Say I Am You*

At the spiritual level we are all the same – essence, pure energy. We came here 'like a star without a name.' We are pure potential. Physically, from the perspective of molecular biology, we are all made of the same stuff, no matter what our color, race, gender, or ethnic background. At conception we are identical.

By the time we are born, physical differences appear and we are subsequently subjected to cultural stereotypes of what it means to be male or female. How do we make peace with this apparent dichotomy of being the same but different? The answer is a spiritual one that I will return to at the end of this chapter. But for a moment let's explore the concept of having gender specific rules on romance, love, and dating.

A huge chasm about having separate rules for men and women is symbolized on my desk. On one side is a stack of dating books by John Gray, Tracy Cabot, Ellen Fein and Sherrie Schneider, Patricia Allen, and others, full of separate prescriptions for men and women – what to do and say to please, attract, and, in my perspective, often manipulate someone into a relationship.

On the other side is a stack of books on Buddhism, Quaker traditions, Sufism, Zen spiritual relationships, and wisdom – by John Welwood, Ram Dass, Krishna-murti, Stephen and Ondrea Levine, and others. None of the books in this stack make separations between men and women. In another tiny stack are my two favorite dating books by Susan Page and Barbara DeAngelis. They truly encourage men and women to be authentic and insightful and to operate with integrity.

My question about any rules or prescriptions for love from a spiritual point of view are these: Do they help people relate from essence – that clear-seeing part of us that is love, kindness and true – or do they limit people and separate them from their authentic self?

Rowan Conrad, a Buddhist student of Thich Nhat Hanh commented: 'The kind of advice in these books seems designed to create what is called "karmic rebound." In solving one problem you plant the seeds for more problems.' For example, if we play hard to get or pour on the charm to attract someone to us, we plant the seeds for anger and mistrust when the mask drops and other parts of ourselves are revealed. Not to mention that we lose ourselves in the process by merging with an image of ourselves instead of being natural and true.

I also spoke with Keith Walker, friend and Buddhist practitioner and psychotherapist about prescriptions for dating. 'It seems to me that it is too often about winning, getting, meeting a desire as opposed to having a genuine living relationship based on honesty and openness. It's kind of primitive. How to entrap someone, how to emotionally pull their strings to make them desire you. It's not about asking, how can I open myself and be in real contact with another human being. Some of them almost seem like a users' manual, but I don't want to be a user when it comes to relationships.'

I also asked Keith about separate rules for men and women. 'Ultimately relationships are about the same energy that gets translated through a different biology. Too much is made of the differences and not enough made of the essence of love. Awareness transcends gender. It's formless.'

We need to present ourselves as we are and as we intend to be in a relationship. Only then can we avoid the Karmic rebound problem.

If someone falls in love with our mask, we have two choices: either we wear the mask and lose ourselves, or remove the mask and risk losing the relationship. The more we present ourselves honestly, whether heterosexual, lesbian, bi-sexual, or gay, the more we will create a spiritual union and find pleasure in being together.

The spiritual lover doesn't want a chase or a competition – he or she wants a lover who wants them back. They want to create a shared union and feel the sweetness of connection.

Aside from the personal gains to be made from having true intimacy, bringing equality to the sexes will help dissolve the fundamental mentality of domination and subordination that has made it so difficult for men and women to meet each other face to face, heart to heart, and spirit to spirit – the foundation for intimacy and love. True intimacy does not appear when we face another as more or less than ourselves. We need to see each other as different but equal.

In the study I made of successful couples for my book *Women, Sex, and Addiction*, I repeatedly found that both individuals in the partnership had a broad range of emotions, including the ability to give *and* receive, be passive *and* assertive, passionate *and* tender, listen *and* talk. They were not bound by sex-role stereotypes when it came to emotions and behavior. They both enhanced each other. Not that they didn't have qualities that were complementary, or experience tension or problems. Of course they did, but the depth of their bond, the shared union of being a couple was so rich it provided the motivation to work through difficulties with utmost respect for each other.

Intimacy requires tuning into our beloved and to ourselves on a moment to moment basis. This creates a spacious fluid quality free of assumptions. In weaving a connection with our beloved, we stay open to the fluctuations within ourselves and our partner. We realize that some people like to withdraw to solve problems, other people like to talk them through. Some people like to do various activities together in silence because words interrupt the stillness and connection. Other people prefer to tell stories or talk when they are together. And nothing is fixed. We may want to be quiet on Tuesday when we walk in a park and feel like talking on Friday. Any time we make an assumption about *all* men and *all* women, or a given person, for that matter, we will be wrong much of the time. In the Quaker tradition we listen for that still, small voice within to guide us. We live in a stream of conscious awareness of the moment.

This way of seeing relationship dynamics is significantly different from John Gray's Mars and Venus perspective. His book is based on stories the culture has created about *all* men and *all* women, stories that reinforce the false core. For example, in talking about the problems strong, independent women have in attracting men and how women need to need men, he writes:

In the old days, a woman was in many ways helpless to provide for herself. She clearly needed a man. This helplessness actually made her very attractive to men and gave a man confidence to pursue her and the sense of purpose and responsibility to provide for her and be supportive.

The image of a man protecting a helpless woman sounds like a parent-child relationship, not one of two equal mates. It is clearly a cultural stereotype that deprives both people of their human potential and wholeness. Inequality of this sort is a prescription for a deadly relationship. In fact, it's not a relationship at all, it's two masks living together. And again, while some men may be attracted to helpless women, it's not healthy to reinforce this idea. As we evolve spiritually, we become increasingly comfortable meeting each other in the richness of our humanness – our talents, strengths, joys, sorrows, fears, neediness, and longings.

Gray, along with other writers, provides numerous lists of specific things to say and not say to a lover that are daunting. Even if one could memorize all of them, they imply that somehow if we only say or do the right thing, we can make a relationship work. While that might be nice, we all know relationships are more complicated than that. Besides, we are far more transparent than we like to believe. People can sense when we are phony, or 'trying to do it right.'

Keith Walker's comment on following rules for dating is that 'forcing oneself to believe or accept a rule, thought, or model without understanding it, and feeling united with it, is to do violence against the self. It is saying *Someone else knows more than I do about what's best for me*. This immediately takes us off the spiritual path.'

We need to take our cues from inside (do we feel clear and relaxed, or agitated?) instead of obediently mouthing someone else's words. To be natural and authentic can feel awkward or frightening, but it is through this exploration that we get to know ourselves. This doesn't mean we don't listen to wise counsel, or learn communication skills, but they must never be pitted against our own counsel or spirit.

It is better to make an honest mistake and learn from it,

than to follow rote rules that are external to our experience or don't feel authentic.

The poet Kabir wrote 'As the river gives itself into the ocean, what is inside me moves inside you.' That's the image of a healthy relationship. The flow of spirit is within us, between us, around us – binding us together as part of all that is. In any meeting with another person, if you want to enter the flow of the river, you must surrender to truth, detach from the outcome, feel the water wash over you, and breathe in the beauty of living at one with your internal wisdom.

Instead of obscuring our vision with stereotypes, what if we met each other with fresh vision and an open mind, asking:

Who are you?
What do you like?
Am I understanding you well?
What helps you feel loved?
How shall we bring up conflict?

By asking these questions, we honor the unique individual we are with. We get to know them based on who they are, today, rather than on assumptions, stereotypes, projections, or hope. It's simply two of us, looking each other in the eyes, listening, responding, and weaving the special tapestry of our relationship. If you do this you will find out what a bright, shining star you truly are.

10

Practice Loving Kindness to Yourself and Others

The Guest is inside you, and also inside me:
you know the sprout is hidden inside the seed.
We are all struggling; none of us has gone far.
Let your arrogance go, and look around inside.
                                    —KABIR, *The Kabir Book*

Kindness reflects a warm, open heart. When we start a new relationship, our ability to be kind is often tested. Suddenly our potential mate is rude to our best friend, she's late and doesn't apologize, he says he'll help us out and then breaks his promise. We're jolted, disappointed. It's easy to react by being judgmental and self-righteous – *the insensitive clod, the self-centered brat*, we say to ourselves. We might feel hurt and wounded and want to say *I can't believe you'd do something so mean.* When we become critical it's time to back off for a moment and reflect so we don't have two people separated from their hearts.

Kindness was embodied in the words of Jesus of

Nazareth: 'Let he who is without sin cast the first stone.' Instead of instantly pointing a finger at others, we can look inside. We'll find that everyone is inside us, because the whole range of human emotion lives in us. When we distance ourselves from someone else, we create distance within ourselves. This does not mean we should tolerate abusive behavior, it means we learn about ourselves by observing our behavior in relationships.

Other people are constantly holding up a mirror for us to see ourselves. If someone comes to us with their grief, and instead of attuning to them, we start crying, we've bumped into our own unresolved grief. If we are constantly afraid of someone being angry with us, we need to look at our own buried anger. The more we have acceptance and compassion for aspects of ourselves, the more we can relax when others act the same way. When someone is upset, for example, we can remain a compassionate witness instead of feeling compelled to calm them down; shut them up; fix, analyze, or judge them; or push them away.

Kindness doesn't suggest we have to *like* everyone's personality or want to spend time with them. We get to choose people we enjoy. But you don't have to throw anyone out of your heart either. You don't have to fix their hurt, take it away, or give them a patronizing pat on the back. You can simply observe them experiencing their feelings as part of *their* journey – and decide if or how you'd like to be connected with them.

Another aspect of loving kindness is to remember that it's not being free of imperfections that's crucial to relationships, it's being honest about our faults and mistakes. When we accept our humanness we become able to apologize (not grovel) for having been rude, insensitive, or dishonest. Our apology to another is a form of compassion to ourselves because it signifies acceptance. This is at the heart of intimacy. If we are struggling with various fears and foibles, instead of hiding them, we can reveal them, hopefully with compassion and amusement. By revealing ourself we find out if our new friend can join us on the journey.

Meditation on kindness: (You can imagine this or remember to do it when you are in a crowd.) *When you are in a crowd, look around at all the different people. Notice their clothes, faces, hair, sizes. Look at their gestures and movements, noticing if they are loose, stiff, or free. Just take it in, without judgment, as if you were looking at a garden of people. Then see them all as energy fields, the same as you. Just energy. As you continue watching, think to yourself, Every person here has had to live every day of their lives, just like me. They have had to get up every day, decide what to wear, face loss, success, hurt, shame, just like me. Everyone fell down while learning to walk, everyone probably felt anxious the first time they kissed, just like me. Each person has a story to tell. Some of the chapters are heroic. Some of them are about loss, some about fear, some about achievement or joy, just like my story. Then continue to think of them as energy, conceived as an egg and sperm, just like you.*

When you say good-bye to someone or decide not to see them again, remember you are a moment in their story. Make it a story that doesn't leave a scar.

Part 2

AWAKEN YOUR DESIRE:
who are you?
what do you want?

11

Send a Clear Intention for Love

While we are not in charge of the cosmic play of energy that moves through our lives, we can explore ourselves to see if we are sending a clear, unambivalent intention; *I'm here, I'm ready, I'm open.* Whether you realize it or not, you are a powerful electromagnetic field transmitting signals through words, body language, tone of voice, and hundreds of non-verbal cues. This occurs at both conscious and unconscious levels and deeply affects the interplay of our relationships.

Several years ago, after being single for a long time, I spoke with my friend Laura, a psychic and astrologer, of my longing for a beloved companion who could truly join me on the spiritual path. We went out to dinner – natal chart in hand. As she looked at my chart, she said that I needed to remember my vulnerability, and stay connected to old feelings of being hurt as a little child, so they wouldn't get in the way. 'But there's no reason you can't have a lover,' she said tenderly. 'With all the energy you put out in the world, you need to have someone special.'

'But something in me believes I'm destined to be alone,' I said.

'You don't have to be alone. The only blocks are in your mind. Just allow yourself to believe you can be in a relationship. There's no guarantee you will find someone, but at least you will send out clear signals.'

After I returned home, I hiked up the mountain behind my house with Laura's words 'You don't have to be alone' ringing in my mind. At the same time I pondered on the inner force that kept trying to convince me that I was condemned to be alone. I kept saying to myself: it's just my mind. It's just a belief. It's not who I really am. There's no destiny like that.

After sitting for a long time on my favorite mountain knoll, amidst the ponderosa pines overlooking the Bitterroot River in the valley below, I stood up and said loudly, I don't have to be alone. I am ready. Did I believe it? Not completely, but my shout reverberated deeply inside, cracking loose the false core belief that had so tenaciously constricted my mind.

What does all this have to do with Buddhism? Traditional Buddhism has nothing to do with manifesting anything. It involves being immersed in our moment to moment experience, realizing we are not our minds, and making friends with every part of ourselves. My sojourn up the mountain helped me break my identification with my mind – the frightening and irrational belief in some mythical curse or destiny. By starting to dissolve this barrier I became freer to be my true self. While this did not guarantee finding a worthy partner, I could stop getting in my own way.

Later, in re-reading books about the enneagram and

talking with Stephen Wolinsky, it became clear that the sense of being doomed to never finding the 'right' partner was emanating from my false core belief that I'm alone. My first task was to observe the thought when it arose, and remember it was just a thought, a belief, or a conclusion I came to long ago. The second was to recognize the web of related beliefs that surrounded it – all the things I did to either prove my false core belief was true, or to compensate for it.

This leads me to mention another false belief that is prevalent in the new-age culture: if you conjure up an image of the person you want to meet, describe him or her very carefully, set your intent, and 'send it to the universe', you will attract the person you are looking for. I tried it. It didn't work. Lots of people have tried it without success. From a psychological perspective it is a form of magical thinking because it suggests we have some forceful magnetic power over others – as if our thoughts reach out to someone and pull them toward us, and they have nothing to say about it. Besides, if it were that easy, we'd all have wonderful partners by now and dating services would be out of business. This isn't to negate the importance of being clear on the attributes of the person you would like to meet, it means that you recognize the limits of your power. Essentially, you will meet someone or you won't.

Stephen Wolinsky, in a workshop, commented that the belief we have power over others stems from spiritualizing a stage of early childhood development. When we were infants, we cried and our mother/caretaker came. Our baby mind came to the conclusion that it was our cry that brought our mother – which made us all powerful. (If she didn't come we concluded we were defective, unlovable, or it was our fault). The reality is that our caretaker either came or she didn't in response to our cries, but we didn't make it happen. So instead of saying 'It took me five years to manifest someone into my life,' we could more accurately say, I was single for five years and finally met someone, and I'm very happy about that. We don't need to dramatize the situation or make it supernatural. It's just what it is. After all, if people stay active and open, by the law of averages many will eventually find a partner.

Another way of becoming receptive to a loving relationship is through opening your sexual energy. Just as animals come into heat and transmit smells and energy to attract a mate, people need to transmit that they are open to physical love. I hasten to add that this is not just the energy of a sexual high, it is the expansive energy of passionate caring, love, enjoyment, and sensuousness blended with our sexuality. It doesn't mean acting like a Don Juan or a vamp, or having instant sex with someone. You can also awaken your sexuality by making love to yourself – allowing the energy to expand upward into your heart as you take time to luxuriate in the feelings, explore your body, and experiment with different kinds of touch. In other words, you become the lover you want to meet.

How does this fit with the Buddhist notion of not being attached to sense pleasures? We can experience deeply our sensuality and sexuality without becoming hooked on the feelings or getting the ego involved – we need to remember that sex *doesn't* mean I'm loved, I'm important, I'm okay. Rather, sexuality becomes an integral part of our human experience that flows through us and between us, embodied by love and commitment.

We can also make room for a lover in a very literal way using principles of Feng Shui. But remember, as mentioned before, this is primarily a way of helping you feel clear inside. From a Feng Shui perspective you can explore the Feng Shui process in detail through reading books (I recommend Terah Kathryn Collins), attending classes, or hiring a consultant in the field to visit your home.

According to Johna Koontz, a Feng Shui consultant from Missoula, Montana, one can make room in the bedroom for a new love in some of the following ways.

- Clean out your dresser and closet. If someone sees a crowded space, at a psychic level they may feel there is no room for them.
- Have a symbolic invitation for someone to join you in your bed – two nightstands, two reading lights, or two pillows.
- Clear out TVs and electronics in the bedroom, which only serve as distractions.
- Throughout your house, remove sentimental objects from past lovers, and if you are widowed, take any picture of your former partner out of the bedroom. Most people don't want to make love with ghosts looking on.
- Remove clutter from your living space, closets, and basement.
- Think about what symbolizes love and marriage to you. It might be flowers, sculptures, wind chimes, or a beautiful picture. You might place objects in pairs in the bedroom – two candles, two roses, two little animals or statues looking

at each other to communicate your desire to be part of a couple.

Whatever you may choose to do, remember that when you radiate joy and vitality and truly care for the wellbeing of others, you send out a high voltage invitation for love.

12

Seek a True Equal

The objective of two lovers is almost always the same; to find meaning in their individual lives and in their life together.

—PAUL PEARSALL, *Sexual Healing*

According to the I Ching, love relationships thrive when both partners support, trust, and yield to the other partner's path. Adaptability, devotion, and unconditional support given in equal measure to each other bring the essence of equality. Equality does not mean unisex or androgyny, or being the same; rather, it reflects two people who adore each other, and give wholeheartedly from a well-developed sense of self. Men need to appreciate themselves as men, women as women. Whether we are heterosexual, bisexual, gay, or lesbian, we need to come together and be aware of who we are in order to feel a powerful interchange of love and honesty connecting us in a river of spirit.

Our degree of equality can be measured in many ways – money, power, looks, or status. It can also reflect our levels of personal power – the ability to articulate feelings, say what we want, and maintain our values in the face of pressure from others. Equality can also relate to the level of commitment to a spiritual path – a willingness to grow, reflect, and face our fears. But most important, in an intimate relationship it's the *perception* of equality that is a determining factor.

Equality doesn't need to mean that both people earn the same amount of money, have equal status, or are equally good-looking. It means they value each other as equals when it comes to making plans, making love, or making decisions. They have an equal voice. One does not sacrifice himself, or herself, to the other. They adore and appreciate each other equally. They may contribute differently to the relationship, but they are equal in feeling responsible for keeping the partnership alive and growing. (I do have one personal bias, however, which is that to be genuinely equal, both people need to know they can support themselves financially so they know they have the option to leave the relationship.)

The reasons for creating an equal union are many. The first is to release both people from fear. When people feel subordinate or dependent, they start to fear being left by their partner. Then, to prevent this, they start to monitor their words, hold back, and attune to the other person's perceived needs instead of to their own truths. (They also end up harboring an unspoken rage which is expressed covertly – the well-placed dig, 'forgetting' to keep agreements, mocking one's partner, and so on.) People who are in the dominant position fear they are loved only for their wealth, status, or position, and that if their partner were a true equal, he or she would leave.

A second reason for equality is that in a thriving relationship, both people evolve by being mindful of their own behavior. In an unequal relationship, because the subordinate mate acquiesces and complies, the dominant one is never challenged to reflect on him- or herself. There is little or no growth, flexibility, or melting into the shared heart – no forming of the 'us' bond that brings two people into spiritual union.

A third reason for having equal relationships is that inequality usually results in dull, routine, vacuous relationships, because inequality often reflects a desire for security – for settling into well-defined roles rather than expanding our limits. If the energy doesn't flow freely within us, it won't flow freely between us.

Another great reason for equality is that it keeps sex alive. The surest way to dampen passion and sexual attraction is for one person to take on a parent role and attempt to protect, fix, change, or repair the other. Likewise, if one person acts like a child, asking permission and advice and always deferring to the other, there can be no equality. If we want to keep the fire glowing, we have to be free, open, and honest with each other, something inherently impossible when people feel unequal.

Two equal people can become allies in exploring the layers of false beliefs that cover their essence. They can journey side by side, taking off their costumes, revealing themselves completely and moving toward a relationship that flows from their essential goodness.

When we bond at the level of spirit or essence, we

start to taste the sweetness of unity and joy. We feel safe enough to merge with each other, creating a shared body of love that gives us a glimpse into the magnificent oneness of the universe. At this spiritual level of connection we are not only equal, we are the same energy. Our tenderness for our beloved becomes a caress of our own heart.

13

Explore the Ways You Bond

We bond on many levels. From physical appearance, values, interests, talent, and temperament, we feel drawn to someone. The more our connection is grounded in spirituality, the better the chance of a lively, vital relationship.

A spiritual connection is when we relate to each other through our highest, wisest self, with truth, compassion, and an open heart.

To explore levels of bonding, read through the following sections and think back on previous relationships as well as the relationship you'd like to create. On what levels did you bond? What worked well for you? What was missing? Then, as you meet new people, notice at which levels you connect. Often we start with the earlier levels and gradually include more and more levels as we progress toward a spiritual bond. (I have not included sexual bonding here. It deserves a separate chapter because it pervades all levels of connecting.)

1. Physical/material.
2. Intellect.
3. Interests.
4. Values/lifestyle.
5. Psychological/emotional.
6. Creativity/passion.
7. Spirituality.
8. Essence.

As you read over the following descriptions of bonding and the illustrative real-life personal ads, note what levels feel familiar to you. Some people find this exploration sheds light on the difficulties in past relationships. Other people find it an affirmation of what they already know. What's important to remember is that the future is long and the high of new romance is fleeting. In many troubled relationships, people simply did not think through their values, interests, or dreams before choosing a mate.

1. **Physical/material.** There are two aspects to physical bonding. The first, physical attraction, reflects our animal, biological nature and plays a crucial role in keeping the excitement and spark in a relationship, although it does not guarantee a successful pairing. Physical bonding can also be based on images and roles – looks, hair color, status, money, and possessions. We want people to fit our fantasies or scripts. *I want a wife. I want someone with money. I want a woman who is thin, young, and has long hair. I want someone with black hair and swarthy skin.* At the same time, if we remember that our image of an attractive person is simply that – an image – we can step back and be open to people who

92

don't fit our image. If you look through the personal ads, you will see how prevalent this level of bonding is in our culture: *Tall, handsome, moral leader, 174 lbs, 42, desires skinny Christian Woman, age 32–36, with small features and pleasing personality.* Or *Self-confident, 5'6", 29, blond-haired, long-legged woman seeking tall, handsome, financially secure male, age 30–35, for outdoor fun and romance.*

2. **Intellect.** The intellect can be the servant of the ego or the spirit. When our intelligence is the servant of spirit, it becomes wisdom. We explore ideas and teachings in the interest of opening up our creativity, being able to solve problems and contribute to each other. The ideas are the means rather than the end.

When intellect serves the ego, we believe our ideas are *real* and a significant measure of our worth. We use information and knowledge to impress people, defend beliefs, win points, and assert our power. But we can get all A's or teach at a university and lack wisdom or compassion. When the intellect serves the ego, people are often serious, righteous, and distant. *Man, 49, 5'10", 170 lbs, fit, handsome, educated, attractive, well read, curious, successful, financially secure, seeks intelligent, slim woman over 5'4" to share lakeside home.*

3. **Interests.** People often connect initially through shared interests. They belong to a hiking club or meet people at a dance or in a bowling league. Interests can include movies, cooking, hunting, sports events, music, hiking, biking, camping, skiing, travel, museums, dancing, and so on. Shared interests can bring intense mutual pleasure that heightens the joy of being together and makes it easy to plan the weekend or the summer holiday. It can also be a catalyst for keeping the sexual spark alive – the shared exhilaration of hiking,

skiing, listening to a wonderful concert together triggers our passion for making love. If you and your partner's interests are poles apart, you need to ask yourself whether you are willing to do the things you enjoy alone or with other friends. Can you accept your partner sharing many of his or her passions with other people? Will you both have the strength not to sacrifice what brings you pleasure in order to placate your partner? On the other hand, shared interests are a building block but many people are able to negotiate differences in interests. One likes to go rock climbing while the partner loves to stay home reading with no one around. The shared interests heighten a relationship, but unless there is a loving bond couples can fight and be lonely even when at a fancy resort, on a mountain top, or in a French café if they don't have a spiritual bond. *SWM [single white male], 32, likes outdoors, hiking, dining out, horses, movies, camping, and fishing. Seeks someone interested in same.*

4. **Values/lifestyle:** Values, which can be objective or subjective, permeate all levels of bonding. They can be about material possessions, child-rearing practices, lifestyle, eating, religion, or spiritual beliefs. They can reflect the ways we spend time, contribute to our community, and get together socially with others. In addition, values can include qualities such as kindness, openness, honesty, and sensitivity.

We need to be honest with ourselves about the values that matter to us. If someone we are dating does not share with us certain cherished values, we can't ever count on them being there. Remember, there's a long life after the rosy glow of romance fades. What's going to happen when you want to live in the city and have children, and he wants to live in the country and raise goats? What's going to happen if you like hiking and camping and he likes luxurious hotels? If you are immersed in a spiritual practice and your partner isn't interested, how will that affect your daily conversations? Are the differences negotiable or will one of you be forced to submerge your interests and sacrifice your dreams? And which partner will do the accommodating? These may seem like boring thoughts when you're in love, but values run deep and don't change easily. That's why it's important to decide which are crucial and which can be negotiated or are not of great importance. Sometimes even though we love someone, we're not a good match because our values and lifestyle desires are so different it will require enormous compromise on one person's part. *Spirited, country living woman, 32, musician, poet, fit, green, enjoys outdoor activities, movies, surprises. Seeks man with similar interests who values integrity, humor, intimacy, family, community, and adventure.*

5. **Psychological/Emotional:** A healthy psychological bond means we are honest with each other, verbally and non-verbally. Our ability to be honest is related to the accessibility and flow of our emotions, our freedom from all the stories we've made up about ourselves, and our ability to attune to each other, and relate from our essence. Our psychological development also reveals itself in our ability to articulate our needs and feelings, and to not worry excessively about our partner's reactions to us. A psychological bond takes time to develop. Through shared experiences, we start to know each other's habits, joys, and passions. We become adept at making plans and settling differences. We treat each other tenderly, resisting all urges to exploit our knowledge of the other's weak spots. *Adventurous SWM, 49, 5'7", stable, professional. Seeks special relationship based on honesty, care, and commitment with someone able to treasure life's everyday gifts. Enjoy hiking, cool jazz, conversations,*

playfulness. Value openness, warmth, honesty, creativity, and humor.

6. **Creativity/Passion.** Creativity is the manifestation of spirit coming through us, permeating our lives with curiosity, fascination, imagination, and originality. Whether it's expressed by making love, playing an instrument, cooking a fish, singing a lullaby, arranging furniture, solving a problem, or fixing things, creativity brings a playful effervescence to a relationship. It's as if two people and their muses join together for the delight and pleasure of mutually creating something they couldn't bring into being on their own. One plus one equals far more than two. Such collaboration can be tremendously personal and intimate because our spirit and soul are revealed through our creativity. *Man, 42, good-enough looking, carpenter, fit, playful. Come sing, dance, play, and revel in life together. Explore the limits of being alive. Enjoy arts, theater, walks, hideaways. Value warmth, kindness, and honesty.*

7. **Spirituality.** A spiritual bond is created through a whole-hearted commitment to completely know ourselves, to be changed, transformed, and affected by another person. *Through the revealed heart we create the shared heart.* Although we are committed to our own path, we surrender to the relationship. There is I, You, and Us. Like two drops of water uniting in the ocean, we exist as ourselves, as a couple, and as part of something greater. A spiritual bond allows couples to drink each other in, to attune to each other's vibration. Often we become telepathic and able to anticipate what the other is thinking or needing.

People with a spiritual union treat their bond like a luminous jewel. Differences or conflict are embraced as something to solve, not cause for attack. The goal is to return to unity, not to win. When loss or trauma shadows their lives, their bond

96

supports them and they can embrace each other rather than creating distance between them. The union is a continual source of gratitude. People give through tender eyes, honesty, kindness, hiding nothing, demanding nothing, and wanting only what is given in love. Just as Jesus of Nazareth said 'Be in the world but not of it,' these couples know how to be *in* a relationship, but not *of* it. They are in each other's hearts, and their relationship is in the heart of the Beloved.

Join me on the magical mystery tour. Spirited woman: art teacher, 43, fit, playful, creative. Seeking like-minded person who values intimacy, integrity, and community to explore friendship, love, spiritual connection. Interests: jazz, classical music, theater, hiking, canoeing, adventure, movies, and cozy cabins. Tell me who you are.

8. **Essence.** Essence is simply being. We live without mind, memory, or association of past experiences or teachings. There is no separation, just a quiet connection to the still center within us that is connected to that great void in the universe – an energy field beyond thoughts, beyond ego. When we relate out of essence we are honest, kind, and compassionate. We see people as they are without projections and idealization. At the essence level we are a steady stream of consciousness, alive to the moment, unconcerned about the past or future. If we were completely centered in this level, we probably wouldn't write an ad. If we did it might say, *Who Am I? Who Are You? Let's explore the journey side by side.*

As we incorporate more levels of bonding – particularly the psychological, creative, and spiritual levels – we come closer to living out of our essence: our masks fall away, fear subsides, and we dance lightly on our journey, relishing the details of the passing moment.

97

14

Fused or Free?:

understanding the path to intimacy

The only way of full knowledge lies in the act of love; this act transcends thought, it transcends words. It is the daring plunge into the experience of union. To love somebody is not just a strong feeling – it is a decision, it is a judgment, it is a promise.

—ERICH FROMM, *The Art of Loving*

No matter how you feel at the prospect of dating – clear and confident, or nervous and tenuous – the task for all of us is the same: to walk the path of knowing who we are, learning to see others clearly, and dropping our images and expectations so we live more from our essence. This allows us to take the daring plunge into union.

Differentiation is a psychological term, first used by family therapist Murray Bowen, to describe the foundation for intimacy. Differentiation means the ability to maintain your identity when you are in close relationship to other people or ideologies: you are able to rest securely inside yourself and not be swept away by other people's emotions, opinions, or moods. At the same time you are open to other people. Differentiation brings a spacious, open feeling, because our mind is free.

Fusion, the opposite of differentiation, is when we become enmeshed with someone. They have a headache, we take the aspirin. They're out of a job, we read the want ads. In many families, fusion is mistaken for love. *If you don't get upset when I'm upset, you don't love me. If you don't want sex when I want sex, you're rejecting me.* When we're fused, differences are seen as a threat because everything has to be either right or wrong. So if we have two different opinions, one person is 'naturally' wrong. This attitude inevitably leads to arguing and blaming. That's why fusion gets in the way of intimacy. It does not allow for two different people with two different ways of thinking, perceiving, or handling situations.

We all started life being completely fused to our mothers. Moving from fusion to differentiation is a *developmental* process that continues throughout our life. In fact, the process of differentiation completely parallels our evolution on the spiritual journey. Spirituality and differentiation are simply two frameworks for understanding the same concepts. I've listed traits of both fusion and differentiation because, in working with clients, I've found that some people like a list that includes red warning flags, while others like a list that maps out where they want to go. In the lists that follow, I lay out the traits of fusion, without much explanation, and follow them with the traits of differentiation. You may find it helpful to read these lists on a daily basis or pick out one or two items to focus on.

As a cautionary note, the ego, which likes categories of right and wrong, might jump to the thought that fusion is bad and differentiation is good. The point of these lists is not to tell you which are the 'right' and 'wrong' ways to act but to help you be mindful on a daily basis. There is no good or bad, simply the *what is* of the moment. We can only change what we are aware of. In Buddhist terms, we could say, don't be attached to where you are on the path, simply bring curiosity and fascination to wherever you are this moment. It's natural to slip and slide between varying degrees of fusion and differentiation given different situations and people we encounter throughout the day.

TRAITS OF FUSION

1. *Losing oneself in close relationships: second-guessing others, monitoring one's behavior to please others, worrying what others think of you.*
2. *Having one's self-esteem/mood infected/affected by other's anxieties and worries.*
3. *Measuring self-worth by external validation – praise, grades, money, status, looks, weight and so on.*
4. *Reacting unconsciously out of childhood conditioning, teachings, or trauma. (We frequently have sudden flashes of fear, hurt, anger, or resentment that are more intense than the situation warrants.)*
5. *Blaming others: we perceive the world, people, and machines as 'doing it to us' rather than seeing our part in the dramas and problems we experience.*

6. *Defensiveness in the face of criticism, different ideologies, approaches, beliefs.*
7. *Needing to be right or always believing we are wrong.*
8. *Being dependent on others to comfort and soothe us.*
9. *Having difficulty giving to others, or giving with an agenda.*
10. *Bonding in righteousness, pain, or as 'victims'. (We portray ourselves as a wounded bird or sorrowful victim of life to invite sympathy or pity.)*
11. *Engaging in compulsive and addictive behavior.*
12. *Changing our persona or behavior to please or control others.*
13. *Rescuing people, worrying for them, being overly dramatic about problems.*
14. *Staying in harmful, painful relationships out of fear and dependency, or fear of being on one's own.*

TRAITS OF DIFFERENTIATION

1. *Maintaining one's center in relationships.* This includes valuing integrity in all aspects of life and being able to define one's self – to say yes, no, and maybe without second guessing our partners' reactions. It also means being able to articulate feelings, take good care of one's self, and be truthful, even when it requires bringing up difficult subjects.
2. *Having one's self-esteem and mood remain constant in the presence of others' anxieties and worries.* We remain compassionate and supportive without becoming emotionally entangled when a friend or loved one is anxious, depressed, or going through a hard time. Instead of absorbing those feelings or feeling responsible to fix the problem, smooth it over, or give advice, and remain a loving witness.
3. *Knowing that one's value is a given.* Our self-worth remains constant in the face of winning, losing, succeeding, failing,

and pain or pleasure because we know our value is inherent in being alive. We are all sacred beings, interrelated to all life.

4. *Developing a set of values through reflection, awareness, learning, and experimentation.* Instead of relying on external authority to determine our beliefs and values, we learn to trust our internal wisdom that comes through experience, contemplation, and meditation. This often means casting off much of what we learned in our families, schools, or religious institutions.

5. *Feeling comfortable or fascinated by different theories, belief systems, and perspectives.* Because we're secure in our own values or beliefs, it doesn't matter if anyone agrees with us or not. Differences are natural, unthreatening, and interesting – they offer a glimpse into another's world. Instead of immediately jumping into our armor – *I do it this way* – we are curious. *How does that belief work for them, how did it get there, what does it mean?*

6. *Recognizing seduction, control, and manipulation – ours and others'.* Spiritual warriors clearly see signs of manipulation and emotional seduction – ours and others'. We don't trust blindly, we trust wisely based on reality. Likewise, we examine our motivations, and don't con ourselves or hide behind phony innocence, charm, or naiveté.

7. *Being able to self-reflect and self-confront.* Well-differentiated people routinely reflect on their behavior and confront themselves. *How did I contribute to this problem, this dull sex life, this disintegrating relationship? Why do I stay with this mean-spirited person?* We keep the focus inward, owning up to our mistakes, apologizing when appropriate and leaving if the other person is harmful to us.

8. *Asking for and receiving support without feeling weak*

102

or compromised. Because we accept our humanness and fallibility, we reach out for help when in need. We realize that by receiving, we are allowing someone else to experience the gift of giving. The acts of giving and receiving join us together in a circle of connection.

9. *Giving without an agenda or the feeling we are giving away a part of ourselves.* Well-differentiated people take pleasure in giving from a place of abundance that is free from score-keeping or hidden agendas.

10. *Seeing others clearly.* As we differentiate, we stop categorizing people, drop our expectations and preconceived beliefs, and get to know them for who they are. This allows us to create true intimacy.

11. *Learning to comfort and soothe ourselves when faced with stress or difficulties.* When faced with anger, hostility, or trauma, well-differentiated people have the inner resources to calm themselves down and step back from the situation rather than reacting impulsively. Instead of leaping into an argument or losing our temper, we can slow down, and not add to the ruckus or descend into someone else's state of turmoil.

Overall, as we differentiate we move from fear to excitement, from separateness to connection, from insecurity to confidence, from seriousness to playfulness and a light heart. We become able to step back and watch ourselves with kindness, curiosity, and a sense of humor. This puts us on solid ground to create a vibrant, enduring relationship. *When we are able to take refuge in ourselves we can merge without fear because we feel whole no matter where we are.*

Thus, in the healthy marriage both partners bring the sum of what they are to the union, and each partner is enriched by the other. In order to achieve this union, each spouse must be open to the other. This was invariably true of the couples I met: they were accessible to each other, readily influenced by whatever the other might have to say. They listened to each other, they watched each other, they took each other in.

—CATHERINE JOHNSON, *Lucky in Love*

15

Define What You Want

*So faith, hope, love abide, these three; but the greatest of
these is love. Follow after love, and desire spiritual gifts.*
                                    —CORINTHIANS 13:9, 14:1

Now that we've looked at these levels of bonding, it's
time to define what you want in a partner. We walk a
subtle line because while we need to have a clear sense
of what's important to us, at another level, we need to
remain open so we can make room for a good partner
who doesn't arrive in the package we imagined.

You thought a great lover had to have hair but you
meet a wonderful man who is bald? Or you wanted
someone who was also Jewish, but this lovely Catholic
woman has you smitten – she's so vibrant, intelligent,
and supportive of who you are. Or you didn't want
someone with children, but these two young daughters
of a man you just met are delightful and you take
pleasure in being with them.

One woman placed a personal ad and received three
responses that interested her. One man mentioned his

utdoor activities – hiking, canoeing, and camp-
Another was involved in numerous community
organizations that she admired; he also shared her outdoor interests. The third, whom she almost didn't call
back, said, among other things, that he ran a motel. She
couldn't imagine they'd be able to connect but something about his voice on the taped message appealed
to her. She met all three, and guess what? She felt
closest to the motel owner. He had inherited the business, and enjoyed it because it gave him free time to
pursue his own interests. He was generous in his service
to the community, enjoyed outdoor activities, and most
important, he had a kind and loving nature. When she
could step back from her preconceived images and into
the experience, she discovered he was truly a pleasure to
be with. And he turned out to be 'the one.'

SUGGESTION:

Keep an open mind and allow yourself to be surprised.
At the same time, remember your cherished values.

Here's a summary of the ways people bond, as discussed
in Chapter 13.

1. Physical/material: looks, status, age, education, money.
2. Intellect: level of intelligence, use of intelligence and wisdom.
3. Interests: hobbies, work, leisure time.
4. Values/lifestyle: religion, number of children, child-rearing beliefs.
5. Psychological/emotional: capacity for intimacy, emotional maturity.
6. Creativity/passion: playfulness, talents, level of energy and joy.

7. Spirituality: commitment to a path of truth, integrity, and service.
8. Essence: the ability to flow from love, truth, goodness, and power.

The following steps will help you create a description of the partner you desire.

STEP 1. Without censoring yourself, under each of the above headings, write everything that comes to mind that you would like in a partner. Be honest. If thin, good job, thick brown hair, and no addictions come to mind, write them down. If you want someone who is highly intelligent, plays tennis, is of the same religion, or is interested in hiking, say so. Take time to write down absolutely everything. When you are done, read your list over and reflect on what you have written.

STEP 2. Looking at your list, notice where your focus is. Is it on the material and interest level, or is it more toward a spiritual level? Is it spread through all the levels? If you are very concrete about physical appearance and age, ask yourself why. What does it mean to you if your partner is thin? Why must he share your interest in golf? Why do you want a man with status? Why is it important that someone be conscious of her spiritual journey? Go deep for the answers.

STEP 3. Go down your list and rank each item from 1 to 3 based on the following: 1) crucial, non-negotiable, 2) desired, but not absolutely essential, and 3) nice, but not necessary.

STEP 4. Based on what you have written, write a paragraph describing the person you want to meet. Include values, interests, looks, or whatever comes to you. The purpose is only to describe the other person. Use as many as fifty words, but no more. Remember that most people enjoy movies, eating out, and cuddling, so be as creative as possible.

STEP 5. Now narrow your list to less than ten crucial words. Then five. Then, can you find one special word that transmits the essence of what you want? When Julia decided to place an ad that attracted a kindred spirit, she wanted someone committed to the spiritual path, but didn't want to sound serious. The word '*Namaste*' came to mind: it's a Hindu greeting often used at spiritual gatherings, which means 'I salute the divinity in you.' And it worked. A man who had never answered an ad glanced through the newspaper and felt a jolt when he saw the familiar greeting. It gave him the impetus to pick up the phone and respond.

STEP 6. Imagine spending time with the person you just described in your fifty-word paragraph. Have you considered the values, interests, and qualities you are looking for in a partner?

STEP 7. Write a personal ad based on your list. You don't have to put it in a newspaper, but you might think of it as the practical version of your letter to the universe. Remember, whatever you do transmits a message. When you write your ad, be your most creative yourself.

This exercise brings to mind a middle-aged couple I met at a BMW motorcycle rally. They presented a slide show of their three-year trip traveling together around the world on one motorcycle. They obviously shared great pleasure in this adventure and showed amazing capacity to rest easy when they faced days of delay due to bureaucratic rules or mudslides on a road. Amazed at their ability to spend such extensive time together and seem so comfortable, I asked them if they had met through a shared interest in biking.

'No,' she replied with a laugh. She'd never been on a motorcycle. He was looking for someone with no children to travel around the world with him, and she got to know him, tried out being on the motorcycle, and decided to do it. This underscores the importance of being totally clear about what you want, and being open to something new. He knew exactly what he wanted to do and that he wanted a mate to share the ride. She knew what she wanted in a human being and accepted a complete lifestyle change to be with him.

So remember: be honest about what you're looking for. If it's someone to share a balloon ride, say so. If you want to hike the Appalachian trail, live in a mountain hut or in a classy apartment in the center of New York City, put it out there. No apologies. And if someone knocks on the door with a new idea, don't slam the door before you meet the person.

16

Define What You Have to Give

The next step is to ponder what you *have* to give, what you're *willing* to give, and how much energy you have for giving at this time. Some people might want a 'Sunday gentleman' for starters, some people are looking for companionship or a friend, while others are looking for an enduring relationship that requires time and emotional energy.

The more honest we are, the less confusing we will be to others. Andy answered an ad for a woman seeking a primary relationship. What he didn't tell her on their initial meeting was that he was primarily attracted to her interests in tennis and biking, and while he had a vague idea that a primary relationship might be nice, he had neither the time nor the emotional energy necessary for creating such a union. Needless to say, there was a lot of confusion and hurt when Andy showed a lot of interest in Julia – he really did enjoy being with her – but then kept pulling away after being close or after making love. 'I just want to be friends,' he said, finally. 'I have friends,' she responded, feeling upset. 'Why did you make love to me if you only wanted a friend? I placed an ad looking for a man who wanted a primary relationship – I wish you had told me earlier.' Julia could also have been more careful reading his signals, asking questions, and waiting until there was a solid feeling of commitment before being sexual.

To assess what you have to give:

STEP 1. Refer to the list of how people bond, discussed in Chapter 13, and consider what you truly have to give to a relationship in each category, from physical/material to essence. Go down the list and write everything that comes to mind on each level. Include your shining attributes as well as troublesome behaviors – you have screaming fits, get demanding, tend to withdraw, chatter when you're nervous, feel easily hurt, get possessive, jealous, and so on.

STEP 2. Write a paragraph that describes you – all of you (this could be from two to ten pages long).

STEP 3. Write an ad that you could put in a dating column. Include what you want and what you have to give.

STEP 4. A day or so later, read over what you've written and make any changes that come to mind. Remember, you don't have to be perfect to find a lover. We can all dance with our problematic traits if we step back and see them as 'stuff' – a part of us, but not our essential self.

17

When to Trust the Power of Attraction

Most happy marriages are held together by a powerful and enduring sexual bond – even when partners do not fully realize it.

—CATHERINE JOHNSON, *Lucky in Love*

Attraction is an amazing phenomenon, a wondrous example of a complex interaction of mind and body. You walk in a room feeling half bored, meet someone who excites you, and within minutes your energy perks up, your heart beats faster, your palms start to sweat, and you feel sexually aroused. This is caused by a huge chain of biochemical responses that involves the hypothalamus, sympathetic nervous system, and pituitary and adrenal glands, which work together to release epinephrine – the chemical that makes us feel 'turned on.'

There is much debate about falling in love. You're attracted to someone because he or she reflects your disowned traits, your wounded self, your desire to merge with an all-loving mother or god. While this is part of the truth, it's important to remember that we are hard-wired as a species to fall in love so that we will mate. That's why sexual arousal is such a pleasurable sensation – it was created to ensure procreation.

Because falling in love is an intense biological experience, we often take leave of our neocortex – the part of our brain capable of reason, reflection, and intelligence – to bask in the pleasurable feelings. Unfortunately, our delight in romance and feeling 'turned on' – the epinephrine rush – can lead us to mistake these sensations for love, and start a relationship with no more intelligence than two cats mating. On the other hand, many enduring couples started with intense physical and sexual attraction for each other. They definitely fell in lust before creating an enduring bond.

We need sexual chemistry and strong attraction to create a lasting fire with a partner. Catherine Johnson, author of *Lucky in Love*, a study of long-term happy relationships, wrote, 'Scratch the surface calm of these [happy] marriages and frequently a strong and vibrant sexuality, a clear sexual *chemistry*, soon revealed itself. Certainly many, perhaps most, of these happy marriages began with a strong sexual attraction even if it had calmed over the years.'

While some of us have the luck to feel a strong attraction, fall in love and form a good relationship, others of us need to be a bit more wary of our sexual attractions. We need to check if our hormones are working in concert with our heart and mind.

To decide on a mate, one of the most important decisions we will ever make, we are well advised to ask ourselves these key questions:

Am I attracted to this person out of an adult state, or a child state?

Am I attracted out of spirit, or ego?

Am I operating from hormones or heart, instinct or wisdom, or a combination of all of these?

In our adult state we seek a partner or spouse as a lover, helpmate, friend, and companion on the spiritual journey. In our child state, we want someone to rescue us, make us feel important, and provide security, comfort, or a sexual high. It's from this childlike state that we fall into Cinderella and the Prince fantasies, and have illusory dreams of being 'in love' forever.

Interestingly, according to Paul Pearsall, author of *Sexual Healing*, the biochemical response to constant infatuation, being 'in love,' or seeking a sexual high without an authentic personal connection leads us to produce large amounts of epinephrine, which creates chronic autonomic agitation or feelings of restlessness and nervousness. This, in turn, can result in irritability, fatigue, and the breakdown of the immune system, leading to chronic anxiety and depression. This experience truly is love-sickness. When people get hooked on the epinephrine high and seek only the thrill, just about anyone will do. Pearsall writes, 'Hot reactive sex followed by cool feelings of regret or loneliness can eventually teach our immune system to be as . . . disconnected as we have been in our intimate decisions.'

On the other hand, when we create a mindful, loving, personal connection with another, and we are sexually attracted to that person, our bodies produce the

114

hormone oxytocin, which contributes to feelings of intense closeness, trust, and sensual feelings. Incidentally, oxytocin is the same hormone that is secreted when a mother nurses her baby. According to Pearsall, 'it's the neurochemical of intimate connection that also helps balance the immune system.' It takes a considerable period of time in a growing, reciprocal, loving union for our bodies to stop creating an epinephrine high and secrete oxytocin instead, which means that many people never have the experience of intense intimacy.

When we combine the knowledge of our biochemistry with our spiritual knowledge, we can see that *what is good for our spiritual journey is good for our relationships and for our immune system. There is no separation between the three. It's as if our bodies are begging us to love well, use our intelligence, and be wise in our choices.*

Our thoughts, feelings, cells, hormones, glands, consciousness, tenderness, compassion, sexuality, and integrity are like the pieces in a kaleidoscope interacting with each other, creating the design of who we are and how we feel. The more they come together as an integrated whole, the more we can trust our attraction.

While many therapists and authors of relationship books suggest that the initial fire of a new relationship will inevitably shift into a more settled companionship that replaces sexual attraction, others in the field disagree. If we choose a partner we are strongly attracted to and stay loyal to our spiritual journeys by keeping kind and true to each other, sexual attraction can remain strong. Indeed, it is this strong attraction that helps people see each other's best traits. This adoration for our partner, which helps us cherish each other, even our foibles, helps keep romantic feelings alive. Most of the happy couples Johnson interviewed were still deeply in love, sexually attracted to each other and clearly living in the heart of the Beloved. They had a grace, familiarity, adoration, and unmistakable sexual energy sparkling between them.

18

Free Your Heart:
make peace with your parents

To have an intimate lover we need to 'leave home.' The Christian wedding vow 'forsake all others and cleave only unto him (or her)' suggests our partner must become primary in our life. This doesn't mean we abandon parents (or children), it means we become differentiated from them, a concept I talked about in Chapter 14.

There are two basic aspects to 'leaving home.' First we need to explore the values and attitudes we learned, sort through them, keep the ones that support our spiritual path, and release the ones that block our journey. Second, we need to explore all the conclusions we came to about ourselves as a result of our upbringing. People often say things like, 'I'm afraid of being intimate, *because* my mother was so cold.' This leaves out a crucial step. In reality, we're not afraid to be intimate *because* our mother was cold. We're afraid to be intimate *because we interpreted her behavior to mean* we were unlovable, and then concluded that intimacy was dangerous. We need to challenge the chains of assumptions and conclusions we came to so they stop driving our behavior. Otherwise, we're constantly mis-interpreting our beloved. Our partner says, 'I won't be able to spend time with you tonight,' and we respond, 'You just don't think I'm important.' Essentially we've fallen into a childlike trance and see the other person as the parent who repeatedly ignored us.

Our level of differentiation from our parents generally reflects the degree to which we've made peace with them. To explore your level of differentiation from your parents or primary caregivers, go through the following list, rating yourself on a scale of 1 (not at all true) to 10 (completely true) for the two most significant caregivers in your past (most questions apply if they are deceased). Then, if it's relevant, go through the list a third time, thinking about your adult children. The lower the score, the more you have differentiated from your parents (or adult children). Again, it's important that you not be attached to giving a certain 'correct' response. From a contemplative stance you can say, 'Hmm, that's interesting, how is that affecting my life?'

CAREGIVER 1 / CAREGIVER 2

_____/_____   1. I am afraid to be different from them, disappoint them, or hurt them.

_____/_____   2. I try to be the opposite of them.

_____/_____   3. I am afraid to be honest with them or to say no to them.

_____/_____   4. I still try to get their approval. I still feel bad that I never got their approval.

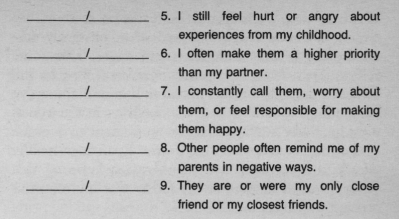

_____/_____ 5. I still feel hurt or angry about experiences from my childhood.

_____/_____ 6. I often make them a higher priority than my partner.

_____/_____ 7. I constantly call them, worry about them, or feel responsible for making them happy.

_____/_____ 8. Other people often remind me of my parents in negative ways.

_____/_____ 9. They are or were my only close friend or my closest friends.

To make peace with our parents is to realize how we are like them, and how we are different from them. We tend to hate in our parents the very traits that we hate in ourselves. We need to make friends with these parts of ourselves. We may even be unaware of these traits and maintain that we are completely different from them. As we become free from the stories we've made up about ourselves, our compassion will spill into our hearts, and also into those giant images called father and mother who slowly become 'that man' or 'that woman,' imperfect human beings trudging on their own path.

Our perspective on our parents' behavior can change dramatically when we penetrate our masks, and see our parents and ourselves with clarity and tenderness. I went from being a rage-filled teenager to an appreciative daughter with regard to my father. It was a matter of clearing out many layers of hurt and anger so I could get down to the admiration and love that were buried. This shift was gradual as I was able to step back and see him as a man with a history, a family, and a heritage. He became a flawed but wondrous human being just like all the rest of us – competent and scared, caring and self-centered, living in a prison of never feeling he had achieved enough. I now remember him and appreciate his kindness toward my friends, our hikes in the wilderness, his lively intellect and encouragement to question everything – except him, of course. I can now look at myself as a teenager with compassion, knowing that sending verbal daggers at my father was my primitive attempt to protect myself.

The key is to tenderly touch our wounds, explore our false core beliefs, and take ourselves and our parents into our hearts where all healing is possible. To forgive our parents is often to forgive ourselves. To forgive ourselves is to forgive our parents.

19

Resolve 'Unfinished Business' with Family, Friends, and Past Lovers or Spouses

Beyond ideas, there's a field. Will you meet me there?
—RUMI

To meet each other in the field beyond ideas, that place of peace and love, it helps to be free of resentment and hurt from the past. For some it's a big task, but as we feel the lightness that comes from clearing the air with others, we gain the courage to continue.

Clearing out old hurts and resolving conflict is both an internal and external process. Sometimes an old relationship still bothers us because we continue telling ourself stories about how it reflects on us – we were a jerk, stupid, or deluded. In this case we need to question our faulty assumptions. There may be no need to speak to the other person. Other times, if the person is currently in our life, or we believe a conversation would be helpful, we might decide to talk with him or her.

In either case, it's important to be aware that unresolved losses and conflict live in us as a form of energy. You may suddenly feel a knot in your gut, a dull ache in your chest, a tightness in your throat when you remember the lover who left without saying good-bye, the time you screamed at your partner and walked out the door, the death of your former spouse, the argument with your brother, to whom you no longer speak. If you notice your body sensations when you think of 'unfinished business,' it will help you realize the cost of carrying this pain around. To become aware of unfinished business in your life, ask yourself the following five questions.

1. Who comes to mind when I think of unresolved grief, hurt, or pain?
2. To whom do I need to apologize?
3. With whom do I need to talk over conflict and seek some form of resolution?
4. To whom do I need to send thanks?
5. What are the conclusions I've made about myself that relate to these situations?

Your list may be long or short. It may also change as you begin the process. You clear the air with one person, and another situation seems to resolve itself in your mind, or you suddenly think of something else you need to address.

If you are serious about a spiritually bonded relationship, take this list and start working through it. While we can sometimes put unresolved conflicts on a shelf, they have a way of falling off and clunking us on the head unexpectedly. We thought we were free from hurt, but when a friend mentions our former lover, we feel a sudden sadness or a sharp burning sensation in our chest.

APOLOGIES

The ability to apologize is crucial to all relationships. Apologies rebuild the bridge that gets severed when we hurt someone else, either intentionally or by accident. Apologies don't require us to grovel or wallow in guilt. We simply acknowledge that our actions were insensitive, unkind, or harmful and say we are sorry. Even if the unresolved situation goes back thirty years, it can be a tremendous relief to make amends.

SETTLING OLD CONFLICTS

First, make a list of people with whom you have unresolved conflicts in your life. Start with the one that seems the most possible to handle. If the conflict dates back a long time, a letter may come as less of a shock than a phone call and give the other person a chance to consider your words and not be caught off guard. It also lets you express yourself with more thought. But listen to your instincts.

The letter or request can be remarkably simple. 'I've been thinking about you lately and feeling a heartfelt desire to meet and talk in the hope of clearing the air. I have no agenda for the future, but perhaps by talking, we can lay to rest old conflicts and at least feel peaceful when we think of each other. With all best wishes.'

If you don't hear from the person in a couple of weeks, you can follow up with a phone call and ask to meet. If the person refuses, you might ask what they *would* be willing to do – talk on the phone? think about it longer?

If the person absolutely won't get together with you, you might write a second letter containing everything you need to say to feel complete. Be direct, don't attack, and try to summarize how you feel without making it terribly long. Imagine how you would feel receiving such a letter. Include:

1. What you appreciated about the person (his sense of humor, the way she supported you in a crisis, etc.).
2. What troubled you or felt hurtful about the relationship. Be specific (his unreliability, her talking behind your back to an old friend, etc.).
3. What you learned from the person and the relationship (the positive aspects – being more responsible with money, learning how to canoe, etc.).
4. Anything else important that comes to mind (perhaps just filling them in on what you've been doing since your last contact).
5. Your willingness (or unwillingness) to keep the door open.

You might be surprised at how effective writing a letter can be. Once I wrote to Marlene, a woman in my Quaker meeting who had suddenly turned cold toward me. I believed that her change in behavior came about because she disapproved of the way I was treating my daughter at a difficult time in my life. In my letter, I briefly explained my concern and asked her to talk with me. Her reply was terse – she sent back my card saying only that she didn't have time, she was too busy. But to my surprise, the next time she saw me she smiled and gave me a big hug. Apparently the fact that I'd brought the 'problem' out into the open had eased her negative feelings toward me. Just like that, the issue was resolved. Marlene and I have been friendly toward each other ever since.

Likewise, if anyone asks you to clear the air, do so unless there is risk of harming yourself. On the spiritual path, we commit to being an instrument of healing and bridging separation. If talking with someone is not safe because they have been violent or abusive, ask for a meeting in the presence of another person, or write a letter.

GRIEVING

Grieving is completed when we can remember a person peacefully, appreciating what we learned from him or her. We no longer feel the gut-wrenching emptiness when we walk into the place where we lived together, or feel intense sorrow when we wake up and remember they are gone.

We need to listen to our inner voice so we don't either rush the process of finding a new person, or deny ourselves the freedom to move on. Traditionally people are urged to wait a year before seeking a new partner – to experience the empty house, the holiday without her, the birthday without him.

Likewise, if you meet someone who is still deeply mourning a loss, you might be wise to step aside and not become involved other than as a friend. A person who is immersed in grief simply cannot enter the flow of give and take with another person until his or her heart is healed. These can be useful guidelines but they are only that, guidelines. Your internal wisdom is your true guide.

GRATITUDE

Unfinished business also includes expressing our love and gratitude to others. So many Dear Ann and Dear Abby letters express regret at not saying 'I love you' before someone died. When we thank people who have touched us in some special way, it's like closing a circle. Someone gave to us, now we give back.

Resolving old hurts and expressing our gratitude allows our energy to flow freely and releases tension in our bodies. I mean this literally. This winter, after I faced some deeply etched fears and dealt with an unpleasant situation that had me emotionally paralyzed, I went cross-country skiing with a friend and, for the first time, I could keep up with her without getting winded. I kept asking, 'Gerry, are you going slowly to be nice?' and she said, 'No, you're going much faster.' Releasing fear had actually improved my wind capacity!

As you begin the process of clearing out unfinished business, be gentle with yourself. In Buddhism, there is no concept of sin. All harmful acts are seen as stemming from unconsciousness and disconnection from our essence. Remember, we're all trying to wake up. When pain exists between two people, it means we're holding onto our illusion of separateness and we can't see through the shell of our personalities to the essence of each other. Once we can diffuse the smoke screen, love often returns, or at least we feel peace, even if we part forever.

20

Experience the Spacious Mind:
observe your limiting beliefs about how people meet

The most important prerequisite for finding a satisfying intimate relationship is wanting one. Wholeheartedly, genuinely, earnestly, singlemindedly, and without reservation.

—SUSAN PAGE, *If I'm So Wonderful, Why Am I Still Single?*

I urge people who are bewildered about why they haven't attracted a lover to explore the negative messages they are transmitting. Many people have a litany of reasons why they haven't met anyone yet – I'm afraid of being hurt again, I pick out the wrong people, there are no good people out there. I'm too old, too young, too fat, too smart, too stupid, too poor, too rich, too opinionated, too passionate, too messed up, too evolved, too boring. Make a list of all your reasons, and then remember they are just that – reasons or excuses.

Listen to your ego protest and then imagine what kind of spaciousness would emerge if your internal Greek chorus would take an intermission, or if you would stop taking all these thoughts so seriously.

To get a feeling for the messages you are transmitting, you might write a mock personal ad based on the negative things you are saying about yourself.

Overweight male, boring, opinionated, tends to get dependent on women, seeks beautiful, talented, loving female to shore up my ego and fill up my emptiness.

Woman, 52, freaked out about being over fifty, worried about my figure, probably more intelligent than most people although I've had a string of painful relationships. Need unreliable man to criticize me and leave after a short time.

These mock ads may sound ridiculous, but whatever we say to ourselves we are transmitting to others as surely as if we walked around wearing a sandwich board sign saying, 'Hi, I'm a mess, come love me.'

We need to remember desperation is different from delighting in the idea of having someone to walk beside us. When we are extremely needy or want someone to fill up our empty life, we will tend to push people away. Even then, needy people do find partners, although it is usually someone equally insecure or troubled.

People find lovers when they are afraid, when they are open, when they are happy, when they are sad, when they are sick, when they are well, when they are looking, and when they are enjoying single life. To some degree it is inexplicable why we meet someone at a given time. In the meantime, however, we *can* make a concerted effort to find a partner but not be attached to the outcome.

The more you meet a variety of people, take part in activities, and put yourself where other single people are, the more likely you are to meet someone. It's the law of averages. When we buy shoes, look for a job, ponder a career change, invest money, or buy a home, we are taught to be systematic and put effort into making a good decision. The same is true for meeting a partner, particularly for those over thirty, who don't automatically meet single people as often as most of us did in our early twenties.

You can let friends know you are looking for someone and you can use ads and dating services or join interest groups. Most local papers list community activities, volunteer work, and various types of support groups. I've known people who met at a crafts fair, on a camping trip, at a Parents Without Partners meeting, at work, through elder hostels, singles tennis groups, a lesbian mothers' group, vocational courses, classes, coffee houses, karaoke bars, sailing clubs, or religious organizations, to name a few. The point is you have to be out in the world to meet people. Occasionally there are exceptions – one friend of mine met her future husband when he came to hang wallpaper in her house – but we can't count on that.

Likewise, we can be open and alert to possible partners without being constantly preoccupied or scanning every event for The One. It's a subtle dance of letting go *and* being open. It's a process, a form of faith, where we play a part but we're not totally in charge. Sometimes we don't find someone because it just doesn't happen, other times it might reflect unconscious ambivalence.

Think of your self-defeating thoughts as a fence around you marking where your compassion ends and your harsh judgments begin. To free yourself, imagine stepping beyond the fence into a vast field that goes on as far as you can see. Allow a breeze to thin out your thoughts and blow them away, and notice that you are part of the vast energy that connects us all.

Part 3

ENTER THE SACRED FIRE:
the journey toward intimacy

21

Crawling in Love:
explore the benefits of staying conscious

One of the biggest mistakes many of us make in looking for the right partner is judging that person too hastily. Sharing your thoughts and feelings with one another may create strong mental and emotional resonance that will spark sexual resonance. Gradual attraction may actually be more genuine than 'lust at first sight.'
—BARBARA DEANGELIS, *Are You the One for Me?*

If you want to maintain your equilibrium and keep a clear mind, or if you've had a history of troublesome relationships, err on the side of the turtle. Go slowly, which is another way of saying 'Be conscious.' Staying conscious can be difficult because our survival instincts want to avoid discomfort and have things defined and settled. But that's not possible in the early stages of dating because there are so many unknowns. You don't know if the attraction will remain. You don't know if the person is as good as he or she seems. You don't know if it will lead to a commitment.

135

Crawling in love is different from falling in love, or in lust, because you stay connected to your intelligence. Falling in love, which is kind of like falling out of your neocortex into your more primitive instincts, can feel euphoric, but it also bears traits of depression – the inability to concentrate, eat, or sleep, being obsessive, not caring about your work and becoming reckless with responsibilities. These signs of depression are not surprising. When we 'fall in love' and project the image of The Perfect One onto our new love interest, it implies that we are incomplete the way we are.

If wild anticipation starts to overwhelm you and your perspective gets foggy, bring your attention to the flow of your breathing. Go inside yourself and ask, *What crazy expectations am I feeding myself? Am I projecting the image of the all-loving mother, the father who will take care of me, the great wedding, or the picture-book life?* Bring yourself back to the present. Peel away your expectations and look at the mortal before you.

Sometimes it seems impossible or completely unnatural to hold back. Keep checking in with yourself. Is this some vague, wild flight of fantasy, or is it the rush of a strong and powerful river? It may be perfectly all right to flow with that strong current so long as you remember:

The only sure path is to live consciously,
moment to moment, as you let go of the outcome.

Some people elect to crawl in love even when their hormones are on fire because, through past experience, they know they can be deluded by strong sexual attraction. Diane told me that after many years of being single, she met someone who sparked her immediate interest, including her old desire to become instant lovers. She told him that she had a history of confusing love with sex and said she wanted to have lots of experiences with him before they became sexual. 'I figured if he argued or pressured me, he wasn't a good person for me. And if he would wait for me it would be great.' They developed a stable bond before becoming sexual and were able to create a good relationship.

Crawling in love is about staying mindful and aware. It also requires mustering the courage to speak from that still, small voice within. It's scary to say 'I care about you' when you're not sure the relationship will work out. It's uncomfortable when your peculiar habits and compulsions are seen. Consciousness carries a bitter-sweet quality of hope and uneasiness. *Staying conscious doesn't preclude the euphoria of an inner tremor when your beloved comes through the door, or the pure joy of spending time together. It means your excitement exists alongside your fears and vulnerability.*

Often couples come for psychotherapy wanting to regain the initial high of romance and sex. They took a flight on gossamer wings and then crashed because they mistook lust for love and never expanded their bond. When we crawl in love we are more likely to find the true fire of hearts meeting because our bond is based on a wide array of experiences, time together, familiarity, and the ability to talk over conflict. Sex and love will flourish alongside the rich, warm feeling that comes from an enduring bond where people dwell in each other's hearts.

22

Using Ads, Dating Services, and Singles Clubs

When you are mate shopping, operate out of a sense of abundance, not scarcity. Deliberately increase the flow of people through your life.
—SUSAN PAGE, *If I'm So Wonderful, Why Am I Still Single?*

I have spoken with numerous people who long for a partner, but are afraid to run an ad, use a dating service, or go to a singles club. Some of their reasons or stories are: 'I don't want to waste my time meeting boring people,' 'I'm afraid I wouldn't know what to say on a first date,' 'I'd hate to hurt someone's feelings by saying no,' 'I'm just not the type of person who would run an ad,' and 'If it's meant to be, I'll just meet someone.'

While no one should do something that goes against their beliefs, if you are blocked by fear but would like to try one of these approaches, here are a few thoughts to help you let go of the stories you create that block you from exploring these possibilities.

- Anything worthwhile takes time and effort. We do a lot of searching to buy shoes, a car, or a house. Why not put at least the same effort into finding a mate?
- Life is short. Why pine away when you can take action to dramatically increase your chances of meeting someone?
- It's an adventure.
- You are not up for auction, you are simply seeing if there's a fit.
- The uneasiness of meeting people through ads or singles clubs will help you meet your edges and grow.
- If you don't know what to say on a first date, you can always say, 'I don't know what to say, I'm kind of nervous.'
- You might meet someone who becomes a friend.
- Finally, what do you have to lose? What do you have to gain?

ADS

Although we don't have arranged marriages in Western culture, you could think of placing a personal ad as a modern version of this practice, with you taking charge of the arrangements. An ad is a forthright statement of your desire. *I'm looking for a friend/lover/spouse, here's who I am, who are you, are you interested?* It's a direct way of meeting people that is inexpensive, accessible, and gets the process started quickly.

Another aspect of ads that can be helpful is that physical appearance is *not* the first step in making a connection. Your brain and intuition get into the act by reading the ad, listening to the voice messages, and having a couple of phone conversations with someone who responds. I am not denying the importance of physical attraction, but connecting at the level of values, interests, and overall intuition can help us see through the surface of another person more quickly.

Ads are especially helpful for the growing mass of people over thirty, forty, fifty, or even sixty, who don't meet many available people on a regular basis. Not only will numerous people see your ad, but by placing it, you are transmitting energy into the universe: *Here I am, willing to take the risk, to plunge – well, maybe crawl – into a relationship.*

Placing or responding to ads (and using dating services) also gives us practice defining ourselves, discerning what we want and setting boundaries – yes, no, I'd like to, I wouldn't like to – the same skills that bode well for relationships. I have placed ads a few times, and twice I met someone who became a very important part of my life. The other time, well, let's just say I learned a lot!

The current trend is to place an ad and leave a two- or three-minute phone message. People respond by reading your ad, and then calling your box number through a 900 number. He or she listens to your taped message and, if so inclined, leaves you a message, including his or her first name and a phone number. You listen to the message and decide if you want to call back. It's amazing what you can pick up on from a short message. Does the voice sound alive, warm, and flowing, or stiff, rehearsed, and tight? Does the person respond to what you say, talk only about himself or herself, or say virtually nothing? Does the message as a whole resonate with you?

If you decide to call someone back you don't have to reveal your last name or give out your phone number. If that seems awkward, remember, you have a right to be self-protective if it feels necessary. Giving up masks doesn't mean we are not careful. Some people feel obligated to return every call and meet every person. While that's a choice, there is no obligation to do so.

When you finally talk with someone, listen carefully to your internal response. What would it be on a one to ten – low to high – rating scale? Keep the conversation fairly simple and remember the point of the phone call is to discern if you want to meet – not to delve into your deepest secrets. Be sure to ask any relevant questions that apply to your bottom line. For example, when I ran an ad, I tried to get a notion of the person's use of alcohol and other drugs because I didn't want to be with someone who drinks on a daily basis or uses drugs. One man became offended and practically yelled, 'I have a right to drink beer after a long hard day. It tastes good,' so I ended the conversation quite soon.

If you can tell there isn't a fit between you and the other person, kindly say so, and don't make plans to get together. Don't waste your time or theirs. Remember, honesty is at the core of spirituality. Most people, myself included, override their instincts and have a few dreary dates before trusting themselves. That's okay, too. You're gaining invaluable skills on this adventure into consciousness.

Singles clubs/Interest groups. There is a vast range of singles groups in many cities. Many of them arrange a variety of social get-togethers and have separate interest groups – singing, hiking, tennis, dancing, and so on. Attending can be uncomfortable at first because, well, people are looking for someone to be with, yourself included. Sometimes it helps to go with a friend initially. If you join an interest group that appeals to you, you will start getting to know people through doing something you enjoy. Don't go with the idea of finding the perfect prince or princess, just go with the idea of having a good time.

Again, the more you get out and practice meeting people, the more you will learn about yourself and what you want. Several people I spoke with said that while they didn't initially meet a mate, they did make some wonderful new friends.

DATING SERVICES

All the same suggestions about personal ads apply to meeting through a dating service. As with the ads, you need to remember that you may talk to or meet thirty people or more before you find a fit.

Dating services vary, but in general, their procedure is to do extensive interviews and give you a questionnaire, which they feed into a computer. They may use pictures or videos as resources. When deciding to use a dating service, ask to see their questionnaire and notice if the questions reflect your values. One time I paid a lot of money and filled out an extensive questionnaire asking me about my interests, my education, physical appearance – all about my life. The only thing they apparently matched me on was height. Every man they set me up with was under 5'5"! Not only did we have nothing in common, we were miles apart philosophically. I called the agency and said, 'Look, I'm a liberal, a feminist. I'm interested in social justice. Is there any way to check this out with people?' They said no, they didn't ask about politics. I asked them to at least match me on something other than height. The next man I met via telephone was a rich corporate executive, who was bent on maintaining our military strength through Star Wars. While I liked his voice and bright energy, we were too far apart philosophically. We had a fairly long chat and I asked him if he was interested in a little book on the human cost of war. He said yes so I sent him *The Hundredth Monkey* by Ken Keyes. I also gave up on the dating service, but that's just one story. Yours could be completely different.

THE INTERNET

Increasingly, there are stories of people meeting over the Internet – some intentionally, some by surprise. One woman, Caryl, who lived in San Francisco, was in a chat room talking about basketball. She loved a remark a man from Salmon, Idaho, made, and sent him an instant message. The two then had a long conversation about sports. Shortly after that he phoned her. A few weeks later he invited her to visit and not long afterward they got engaged and were married.

One couple who met via the Internet sent photos and videos to each other once they felt a strong connection. I urge people who meet long distance to send pictures or videos, because you need to have some idea if there is a physical attraction. Again, it's not a surefire indicator, but you will probably know who you are *not* interested in from a picture. If you're in doubt, and there's a good match on many other levels, see what a meeting brings.

The downside of the Internet is that because the people who meet there often live in two different cities they won't have the opportunity to be together on a daily basis unless one relocates. Because it's so easy to drift into a fantasy world and create the person of your dreams when you are at a distance, a long-distance relationship can be risky. Yet people do meet this way. Anything is possible.

You need to follow your instincts about trying any or all of these approaches. The attitude you bring to any situation will affect your experience. If you think of a singles gathering as a meat market with everyone on the prowl for sex, that will be your experience. If you go with an adventuresome spirit and see the desire for love in everyone, that will be your experience.

As with everything, you need to keep stripping away the layers of your expectations, projections, and hopes so you meet people without having past filters and memories clouding your vision. Keep asking *Who is this person right now? Who am I right now?*

Overall, with ads and dating services, remember not to get attached to the outcome, but simply see it as a way to open the field, and put your intention out into the universe.

23

Remember, First Dates Are Just a Moment in Time

When a man and a woman who are destined to marry happily meet, they feel right together almost at once. Certainly they experience no dark undertones – it is an experience flooded with daylight.
                    —CATHERINE JOHNSON, *Lucky in Love*

A first date is arranged. It might be with a casual acquaintance or a long-time friend in whom you suddenly became interested romantically. If the date was arranged through a dating service or a personal ad, it will be the first time you two meet.

On the spiritual path of equality, the man or woman can initiate the meeting. I know this breaks one of the primary rules of many dating books, but *if we are going to create love and respect between the sexes, we need to make dating a model of equality.* Besides, at a spiritual level, there is no difference between men and women.

If you are meeting someone you already know, let your instincts be your guide, although I'd avoid going to each other's home unless you know the person well and have been there many times. Even then, I recommend caution, because when friendship turns to romance, people sometimes change suddenly. If it's someone you've never met, make simple plans to be together for no longer than an hour and a half – coffee, a casual lunch, a walk in a public place, or whatever evolves from your conversation. If you make a good connection, you can spend some additional time together. Remember, always meet in a neutral place with lots of people around, dress as you usually do, and realize that if you want to feel liked, you have to show who you truly are. *If you present an image, and that's what they fall in love with, then you'll be stuck trying to maintain that image.* And you won't have an authentic relationship or feel loved because it's your acting job they liked.

Don't spend hours fantasizing or getting yourself wound up in expectations. Remember, you may meet numerous people before you find a worthy lover. At the same time, remember, no one is the 'wrong' person, they are just not what you want. Let each meeting be a window into someone else's life, a shining moment rising up, the *what is* of your adventure.

Here are some thoughts to help you relax: You are simply meeting to see if there is a possible fit. You are both sacred people on the path, both seeking love. It's all just a moment in time, a glimpse into another's life, a lesson. You are not being auctioned off. No one is right or wrong, desirable or undesirable. It's a matter of seeing if there is a connection. You can't force a connection. It's either there or it isn't. No one can reject you except yourself. Be true to yourself. If you are not inclined to meet a second time, say so. If you know you'd like to get together again, say so. If you are disappointed that the other person doesn't want to see you again, know it was not in your best interest in the long run.

Remember that most often, a first date is a time to decide if you want a second date. You gather data: *Am I drawn to this person? Do we have common interests or values? Is there a flow between us? Do I feel comfortable being myself?* Let it be simple.

I have read countless books on dating, all full of rules about what to say and not say. But the truth is this:

On the spiritual path the rules are simple.
Be kind, compassionate, honest, and natural.

Let yourself tune into the experience. Notice the process of arriving at decisions. How do you decide who pays, for example? Some men immediately pick up the tab. If it's two women or two men they are more likely to split the cost, although not always. If I know I won't see the person again, I prefer to pay for myself. One time I asked a man if he wanted me to help pay for dinner and he said indignantly, 'I'd *never* let a woman pay for her dinner.' What else would he *never* let a woman do, I thought, knowing in my heart that this could never work.

When Julia met Tony, the man who responded to her ad that started with the word *Namaste*, they had such a good time at lunch that they ended up spending the rest of the day together, running errands, walking, having dinner, and attending a jazz concert. She was taken aback at the concert, however, when he bought himself a ticket and turned to her and asked, 'Are you okay going dutch?'

'I said yes,' Julia told me, 'but I could feel the feminist inside me arguing with the romantic who wanted to be treated. But why should he pay more than I do? I knew he didn't have a lot of money. I wondered if it meant he was stingy. Before the second date we talked over "who pays" and agreed that we would take turns paying for each other, because I don't like the separateness of going dutch. I much prefer the flow of giving and receiving.'

If you get caught up obsessing about the other person's response to you, remember, *there's a fit or there isn't and you are who you are*. We are far more transparent than we'd like to believe. Of course, it's a good idea to listen well, respond to the other person, reveal something about yourself that's not too personal, and have a sense of humor. But if you've never listened well, you tend to chatter or you're usually serious, that's probably how you'll be. You can pretend to listen, or make encouraging remarks, but if it's not heartfelt it will seem plastic.

So if you are naturally outrageous and funny, be that way. If you are naturally cautious and quiet, be that way. If you are great at drawing someone out by asking questions, do so. Being yourself is an act of faith and self-love, and the only source of an authentic union that takes us beneath our masks so we can know each other.

Another way to raise your awareness is to notice the level of energy between you. You could again take a meter reading on the level of connection, rating it from one to ten, with ten being high. What's the energy level when you talk about your interests? What happens to the energy level when one person talks on and on? What happens when one of you complains about a past spouse? If your energy drops and the conversation gets dull, change what you are doing, even if it means interrupting and redirecting the conversation. Sometimes it helps to say, 'I'm feeling awkward,' 'I'm not quite following you,' or 'I don't know what to say,' or even, 'We don't seem to be connecting very well.' Paradoxically, any authentic remark of this sort will usually liven things up . . . or help you realize there isn't a fit.

Toward the end of the first date, you can decide if you want to meet again. Either person can take the first step. You can pose a question: 'Well, where do we go from here?' or say, 'I'd like to see you again, we seem to have a lot in common.' On the other hand, if you decide you aren't interested, don't lead the person on. Don't say 'I'll call you' if you don't truly mean it. If someone asks why you don't want to make another date, you can say, 'I don't think there's a fit' without giving reasons. If the other person uses pressure tactics, it's time to extricate yourself.

If there are dark undertones starting on a first date, step back. Even if you feel only a wiggle of doubt that keeps popping up, or a distant chime in the back of your head, listen, listen, listen – especially if you have a history of denying trouble. When we start to fall in love, especially if we become sexual right away, warning signs may be hard to hear, but remember, early harbingers of trouble usually came home to roost. As a couples' therapist, I have seen repeatedly that the misgivings felt on the first few dates still permeated the relationship twenty years later. As Catherine Johnson writes, a good relationship feels 'flooded by daylight.'

If you both agree to see each other again, either make plans or arrange a phone call. It's also okay for you to say you're not sure of your feelings, but you'd like to meet again. In some cases people realize they aren't attracted as lovers, but would like to share common interests as friends.

Remember, on the spiritual path we don't 'do it right,' we do it naturally, with curiosity and a light heart. Of course we have hopes, but, on the path, acceptance is paramount. Put forth an honest effort and let go of the outcome.

Here are four suggestions to keep you on the path:

1. Stay tuned into the level of connection.
2. Notice the flow of give and take.
3. Trust yourself and your instincts.
4. Have fun, and remember, it's all a passing show.

24

Children and Dating:
enough love for all

You are the bows from which your
*   children as living arrows are sent forth . . .*
Let your bending in the archer's hand
*   be for gladness.*

                         —KAHLIL GIBRAN, *The Prophet*

If there were ever stories of torment or love, they can be told by children of parents who remarry or take on new partners.

While we frequently hear stories of stepparents being jealous and rejecting of their stepchildren, there are also many situations when children find a loving ally in a stepparent or the new partner of their mom or dad. Other times children are initially resentful, but with time they come to form a trusting bond. With all blended families, parents and children need to define the situation and allow everyone room to explore and express their concerns and fears.

We are all the keepers of our children – we owe them

protection, safety, and love. Our insensitivity and reckless decisions can become painful legacies that severely impact their lives. On the other hand, if we give our children understanding and consideration and maintain a loving bond, they won't have to build walls around their hearts to shield their hurt, and they can even thrive when a parent becomes involved in a new relationship.

It's crucial to be honest with ourselves when becoming involved with someone who has one or more children at home. Are you willing to share your partner's love with the children and allow them into your heart? Or do you feel you are through raising children, or have no interest in helping rear children? Do not judge yourself either way, just be completely honest.

If you have children, tread carefully when bringing new people into your life and consequently their lives. It can be unsettling for kids to see a string of people swoop in, then suddenly disappear. If a prospective partner is jealous or hostile toward your child or children, stay away. This is not a good person for you or your family.

There is a fine balance between loyalty to one's children and loyalty to a new partner. Children are highly attuned to signs of being ignored or demoted to second place. What they usually want is a clear but simple explanation of what's going on. You can talk with them about new friends and assure them with words and behavior that they have a safe place in your heart. After all, if you are single, it's likely that they have already suffered the loss of one full-time parent whether through divorce or death. The thought of it happening again may terrify them.

At the same time, you are the adult. You don't need to justify going out – if you feel you do, it's usually because of your own guilt. Just help your child understand the situation. 'This is a new friend. We're going out for the evening. I'll be home later, and we can have breakfast together tomorrow morning.' When we don't give our children clarification, they may well ask for it at an awkward moment. I remember my daughter, in her innocent little voice at age four, asking a first date, 'Are you my mommy's boyfriend?' And worse, 'Are you going to spend the night?' Better I had talked to her first!

A child with a secure, loving parental relationship is more likely to welcome a parent's new love interest than a child who feels emotionally starved or has been the parent's primary source of intimacy. In healthy parent-child relationships the roles are clear and parents don't use children for their primary intimacy needs. Securely bonded children will often see the possibility of more love when a new person enters the picture, while insecure children will fear that the new person will take love away.

Mark, a widower at age forty, had two daughters, ages eleven and thirteen, who encouraged him to date, totally trusting the safety of their bond. They wanted their dad to be happy and were excited to meet his new friend, Judith. Judith, feeling welcomed into the family, took delight in her new relationship with Mark's daughters. One time she took them to a crafts fair where they made masks together, something they had never done before. Their father also spent special time with both of them apart from Judith. They never showed jealousy and everyone's life shone a little brighter.

Some single parents told me they decided to stay single until their children were grown. One woman said she thought it would be unfair to bring a 'stranger' into their children's lives. But fairness is not an either/or situation. It's our ability to choose wisely – to balance being a good lover and a good parent. A dear friend of mine, a single parent of three young children, met and married a wonderful man who became a much-desired father figure. It was a tender moment when the youngest child came to him and asked, 'Can I call you Daddy?' In this case, once again, the circle got bigger for everyone. And that's the crucial issue. If we partner with a helpmate, lover, and friend to our children, life gets richer and easier. If we pick someone who upsets the family ties, and takes energy but doesn't give back, life can become far more difficult.

> *Your children are not your children.*
> *They are the sons and daughters of Life's longing for itself.*
> *They come through you but not from you.*
> —KAHLIL GIBRAN, *The Prophet*

25

Notes on Same-Sex Dating:
free from the rules

I, you, he, she, we
In the garden of mystic lovers,
these are not true distinctions.

—RUMI, from *Say I Am You*

In Buddhism, commitment and loving are most important
in relationships. Our path is not to judge, rather to realize
when our actions are harming ourselves or others. This is
true for all people – gays, lesbians, and heterosexuals
alike. We are all sacred people on the path of awakening.

—ROWAN CONRAD,
BUDDHIST MEDITATION TEACHER

The wonderful aspect of same-sex relationships is the
freedom to chart new ground in moving beyond sex-role
stereotypes and the inherent power differences of being
male or female in our culture. Because stereotypical
male-female rules fall apart in same-sex dating (and I
hope they will fall apart for heterosexuals as well), there

are no limiting rules about being receptive or giving, assertive or passive, or having one person always pay for the other. We're two people, free to relate to each other as individuals, asking, 'Who is this person?' 'What does she like to do?' 'What makes him happy?'

Paradoxically, as a bisexual woman I have come to better understand men through my relationships with women. I've had to explore all the roles ascribed to men. Because there's no man to take the lead in a lesbian relationship, I've had to share the responsibility for taking a relationship forward and feel the discomfort of reaching out a hand not knowing if it will be refused. It's given me a deeper comprehension of why men layer over their fears with a tough exterior – it's not easy to play the role of initiator and repeatedly risk having someone say no.

When I read numerous books on dating, none of which mention gay or lesbian people, I amused myself imagining scenes of gays and lesbians attempting to follow their rules. For example, if two gay men observed the rule 'Don't Talk to a Man First,' what would they be expected to do? Make gestures or wink at each other? What would it be like if two lesbian women accepted the theory that women should show only 'receptive interest'? Would they both just stand around waiting for someone to give?

The troublesome aspect of being gay, bisexual, or lesbian that has a profound effect on relationships (and living and feeling alive for that matter) is internalized homophobia, or trying to live in a world that is so extremely uncomfortable with gay and lesbian people and does not create equal rights and protection under the law in most places. Homophobia means the *irrational* fear of homosexuality. Internalized oppression applies to taking in a negative stereotype about oneself, believing it, and turning it against oneself. A parent repeatedly calls us stupid and we start to believe we are stupid and act accordingly. In the case of homophobia, people sometimes take in stereotypes of being weird, defective, shameful, and wrong, and turn those stereotypes against themselves. The next step of internalized oppression is turning our negative belief on someone just like us. If I'm bad to be lesbian, then you're bad to be a lesbian. This obviously wreaks havoc in intimate relationships. For this reason, gay and lesbian relationships have the potential to be more fluid and loving when we accept our sexual identity and have good support from friends and family.

At a pragmatic level, if we keep our identity a secret, it's hard to meet other lesbians or gays. We spend a lot of time feeling uneasy, wondering when and if to broach the subject with someone we guess might be gay or lesbian. At a deeper level, being 'in the closet' is completely contrary to the spiritual path, because it is a profound denial of who we are and automatically means being embroiled in a web of secretiveness at work, with family, and friends. We refer to our lover as our housemate, we meet down the block after work so we won't be seen by our colleagues. We don't touch in the movie house or go to the office party together, and holidays with families are superficial at best. We constantly hold back, which starts to build armor around the heart.

When people are not part of a supportive social

network, the resulting isolation puts stress on a relationship. All couples need to be supported in their bond and be friends with other couples. Being 'in the closet' keeps us constantly focused on our identity as a lesbian or gay person. On the other hand, if we are with others who have accepted our sexual orientation, or are part of a supportive spiritual community, and there are many, then we become just Judy, Andrew, Michael, Yolanda, Martha, Ruth. We're not fixated on our lesbian or gay identity; we're friends, joined in community, talking, getting to know each other, sharing our stories.

To have a positive relationship, reveal yourself as much as possible – with gay and lesbian friends as well as heterosexual friends.

Of course, there is an art of timing to revealing one's sexual identity, and there will be situations where it's either unimportant or would be self-destructive. On the other hand, when we hide our identity, not only are we isolated, our internalized homophobia takes root and grows. Relating back to our original discussion of differentiation, 'coming out' is part of the process of differentiation – separating ourselves from others' prejudice.

We can't change who we are – our basic nature, our temperament, our passions. We can only become more truly as God or Spirit created us. This is true for all people – lesbian, bisexual, heterosexual, and gay. The more truly we are ourselves, the more we live from our essence, the more deeply we can bond in a relationship. And all love is God's love. It's that simple.

Recently, I attended a workshop on 'coming out' led by Chastity Bono. She engaged the audience through a series of questions – When did you first come out? What happened? What was the response? Do you regret it? While there were many stories of family uproar and heartache, *no one*, repeat *no one*, said they would ever go back in the closet again.

Most of us are in the closet about something – we still harbor secrets we've never told anyone. This whole book is about coming out of the closet and revealing our fears, hurts, shame, pain, joy, talents, and passion. And coming out is not a one-time event: the spiritual path is one of revealing ourselves daily. It is about self-knowledge, openness, acceptance, and love. It's about seeing that spirit and goodness in everyone.

26

When the Buddha Makes Love:
sexuality, spirituality

*There is nothing like making love with the Beloved.
Nothing like the boundary-less heart to make us edgeless
and agile.*

—STEPHEN AND ONDREA LEVINE,
Embracing the Beloved

The first step in making love is for both people to
feel sexually and emotionally attracted to each other.
This may seem completely obvious, but it's amazing
how many people deny their lack of sexual attraction
because they want the comfort, security, and companionship of a relationship.

According to Stephen Wolinsky, 'If you put sexual
attraction on a scale of one to ten, where ten equals
"you can't keep your hands off each other," five equals
"you can take it or leave it," and one equals "repulsed,"
to support a vibrant relationship it should be at least a
seven, preferably an eight, nine, or ten. With work, you
might raise the attraction one notch, but because there

is so much biochemistry involved in sexual attraction, it's hard to do much more than that.' So if a sexual attraction doesn't evolve, remember, it's not anyone's fault, it's just the *what is* of your pairing, and you might make better friends than lovers.

Sexual attraction doesn't have to be instantaneous on first meeting, but it must eventually flower because it provides basic glue for a successful conjugal union. If we're not sexually alive to our beloved, it often leads to a subdued relationship, loneliness, affairs, or lots of fantasies.

No matter how old or young, gorgeous or plain, experienced or inexperienced you are, initiating sex with a new partner is charting new ground. *Do I take her hand? Let my glances linger? When do we first kiss? How do we kiss? What do we say?* There's the freshness and newness of *this* body, *these* kisses, *this* touch, *this* smell. Sexual union can be an exquisite dance of attuning to each other, becoming vulnerable and revealing ourselves.

Sexual intimacy requires that we transcend sex-role stereotypes and embrace all human emotions. When we both become giving *and* receptive, wild *and* tender, playful *and* still, there are more variations to the dance. We meet each other in the richness of our humanness, not as caricatures of men or women. At a spiritual level, there is no male and female, rather there are two people flowing from essence, embracing through their physical bodies.

> *The power of Love came into me*
> *And I became fierce like a lion,*
> *then tender like the evening star.*
>
> —RUMI, from *Like This*

Spiritual and cultural attitudes toward sexuality are very confusing. At one extreme, celibacy is often taught as the path to God. Yet celibacy, if it is externally imposed, is just another attachment, and while it can be part of one's spiritual path, it can also deny a powerful biological and emotional form of connection.

The thing called passion has to be understood and not suppressed or sublimated . . . To love is to be in direct communion . . . how can you love and understand passion if you have taken a vow against it? A vow is a form of resistance, and what you resist ultimately conquers you.

—KRISHNAMURTI, *The Book of Life*

There is no reason that anything so potent, natural, and human as sexual love be placed outside the circle of spirituality. And there is no reason that celibacy should ever be seen as a 'higher' spiritual state than two people with a heartfelt connection making love to each other as the Beloved.

This is not to say all sexual contact is in harmony with spirituality. Unfortunately, many people become obsessed with sex, using it in a desperate attempt to create a bond they are unable to feel emotionally. They confuse sex with love, power, and control. It becomes a source of alienation and takes us further from intimacy. The spiritual path is one of balance and being at peace with all of who we are, which certainly includes our sexuality.

It's important for people in a new relationship to explore the *meaning* of sexuality and lovemaking. What does sexuality mean to each of us? What are we committing to when we agree to be sexual? We can ask ourselves if we are being guided by ego or spirit – the ego seeking a physical high or using sex to capture a partner, as opposed to the spiritual desire to know each other more truly and enter deeply into a flow of giving and receiving.

At a spiritual level, making love is an experience of the shared heart that flourishes alongside honesty, love, and commitment. It flows from knowing each other well and desiring to dissolve into the heart and body of each other. It can't be learned through a how-to manual, or instruction book, because it uniquely reflects all of who you are. If our bodies and hearts are armored, we may need counseling or body work to loosen the physical and emotional walls we have constructed. Otherwise, we're not present when we have sex and we are unable to connect. When sex is devoid of a free flow of energy, it becomes empty and can start to feel aversive.

When we don't find meaning in life, we seek stimulation instead.

There is a lot written about how to have more intense orgasms. While there is nothing inherently wrong with wanting a more exciting orgasm, if we focus on orgasm because there's nothing else bonding the relationship together, the orgasm will never satisfy, no matter how wild and intense. It's the same as using pornography, pin-ups, or fantasies of other women or men to become aroused. There will be more and more need for superficial intensity because the sexual act is devoid of meaning or genuine connection.

Even so, many of us – dare I say most of us – have given in to raging hormones or fallen madly in love, and disregarded common sense. While this puts us in an illusory world of believing our partner is responsible for our bliss, there can be magic in these encounters. We feel drunk with love (which is actually caused by hormones in the brain that create an amphetamine-like high), break our shells, and for a moment touch the divine experience of union with another. It gives us a taste of what's possible with an abiding, honest relationship. With age and experience, we surrender in a different way – to the deep, enduring stream that runs below the wild surface of the river. We want something passionate *and* steadfast – something grounded in reality.

When I asked people what opened the path to free-flowing sexuality for them, the most frequent word they mentioned was *trust* – trust in oneself and one's partner. Trusting ourself means knowing we will voice our desires, define what we want, and have the will-power to leave a situation that isn't right. We trust our partner to be caring, responsive, nonjudgmental, willing to talk, and above all, to respect us whether we say yes or no. Sexual love that combines body, mind, and heart helps us create and re-create our connection, exploring, opening, and freeing our bodies to do what they want to do.

Becoming natural and free with sexuality is a developmental process of experience and experimentation. David Schnarch, author of *The Sexual Crucible*, commented at a workshop that many couples limit their sexual experience by the covert agreement – 'I won't ask you to do anything that makes you uncomfortable if you won't ask me to do anything that makes me uncomfortable, and we'll only do what's left over.'

As mentioned earlier, it's important to remember that nearly all new learning and experimentation are accompanied by anxiety or discomfort. Most of us can remember thinking 'yuck' the first time we heard of French kissing, oral sex, and so on. But when our heart and hormones started to connect, well, what a different experience. We need to repeatedly break through barriers to be able to relax into lovemaking. Our willingness to stretch, grow, experiment, and take risks brings vitality to our daily experiences as well as our sexual relationship.

I interviewed numerous couples who initially fell in lust before developing a lasting bond. I also interviewed numerous people who had come to the conclusion that falling in lust can lead to a lot of pain and misunderstanding. They had decided to get to know someone first and have a commitment. Because sexuality creates a powerful high, it's incredibly easy to get entranced with the biological feelings and lose perspective on the relationship.

While some people argue that being intentional about sex kills the spontaneity, we need to remember that worry, anxiety, and ending up with venereal disease, AIDS, or an unwanted pregnancy are the real killers of spontaneity. Also, without commitment, we often feel the anxiety of the nagging thought 'Will s/he still be here tomorrow?' whispering in our ear. And that kind of anxiety does not make for true lovemaking.

The timetable for becoming sexual is largely internal – meaning it's a decision of head, heart, and hormones. Both people need to feel ready, trusting, and able to look each other in the eyes while making love (without the use of alcohol or other drugs).

Here are some questions to explore before becoming sexual with a partner.

1. Have we talked about venereal disease, AIDS, birth control?
2. Have we managed some conversations about what's going on between us, how we are doing and feeling, and what we are afraid of?
3. Have we handled some level of conflict and acknowledged differences?
4. Is there a balance of giving, receiving, and initiating plans?
5. Are we able to make good eye contact while talking about difficult subjects?
6. Have both of us revealed vulnerable aspects of ourselves and felt respected and accepted?
7. Do both of us feel safe to voice our preferences or accept our partner saying yes, no, a little more, a little less, or not now but maybe later?
8. Are we comfortable touching *and* exchanging spontaneous hugs and other expressions of physical affection throughout the day?
9. Have we talked over our level of commitment to each other?

The first sexual encounter with a new partner may be wild, passionate, unremarkable, or frustrating. Like the waxing and waning of the moon, the rising and falling of the tides, there is a rhythm to our passion and lovemaking that evolves over time. Sometimes we break through for a moment, and let ourselves feel desire, but then old memories flood our mind and we go back into our shell. This can be a time of self revelation, if we're willing to explore the meaning associated with our fears or tendency to shut down sexually. It can also be a time to reveal ourselves to our partner.

Whatever we experience sexually reflects part of our Buddha self because our Buddha nature embraces all experience. We are Buddha kissing with all our heart, Buddha pleasuring a partner with complete joy, Buddha going numb, Buddha feeling afraid, Buddha enjoying orgasm, and Buddha feeling union. It's all experience, and it all carries the potential for awakening.

27

How to Find Yourself When
You Lose Yourself:
take refuge in the Buddha

*The only true joy on earth is to escape from the prison of
our own false self, and enter by love into union with the
Life Who dwells within the essence of every creature and
in the core of our own souls.*
—THOMAS MERTON, *New Seeds of Contemplation*

When we stop being true to ourselves, we fall into
the prison of our false self. From giving away too
much money, time, and energy, to worrying, to ignoring
friends, to repeatedly asking our partner, 'Are you all
right?' to buying too many thoughtful gifts, to faking
understanding, we slip off the path of truth and don the
costumes of various personas – helpful, suave, charming,
elusive, successful, cheerful, competent.

We pick up the phone and put it down six times,
knowing we shouldn't really call again. Then we lose
control, dial, and are speechless when our friend

answers. We try to be chatty and pleasant because we're too embarrassed to say, 'I'm worried you're leaving me.' Our stomach flutters. *Will she go back to her old boyfriend?* Our world shrinks. *I've got to keep this man, I've got to play my cards right.* We panic. We're suddenly frightened by our past, worried about the future, and totally out of touch with the present.

What's really happening here is that we are slipping off the path and driven by our false core beliefs that say, 'I'm alone, I'm incompetent, unlovable, inadequate,' and so on. To hide from these painful feelings we often do things we know are ill-advised. If you get anxious or start to panic, it's time to realize that your emotion-backed demands have dumped mud over the jewel of your perfect self. There is much to be learned when we hit these edges. Here's an internal chat Julia had, as she imagined talking with the Buddha.

'I'm so worried about keeping this man,' Julia says, as she pictures them sitting together under the Bo tree. 'He's the best thing to come along in years.'

'Have you noticed the beauty of leaves on the tree?' Buddha says.

'Buddha! What the hell does that have to do with what I'm saying? I'm upset. I need help.'

'Help for what?' Buddha says.

'To feel better?' Julia says.

'How about being exactly where you are?'

'Why in God's name would I want to keep feeling this way?'

'Because it's a part of you – a part that needs your awareness and compassion.'

'But what about Tony, what should I do?'

'You need to come face to face with a truth about yourself. There is a big empty place you're trying to fill up with this man. You're clutching to this relationship to feel secure, but security comes from completely letting go of all control and allowing yourself to feel whatever you fear. You are trying to create solid ground under your feet so you don't have to experience being alone, but if you would let go, you'd find that the emptiness you fear is really a still and restful place.'

'But what do I do with this anxiety?'

'Do nothing. Sit with it quietly, feel your breath. Then ask yourself the truly important question: Why are you so afraid of someone leaving you or of being alone? Be more honest. It's the only refuge you have.'

There is an expression, 'take refuge in the Buddha,' meaning take refuge in your own true and perfect Buddha nature. Our refuge is in being exactly where we are – not dramatizing our problems by replaying them in our heads, telling stories to our friends, eliciting sympathy and convincing ourselves that this is a very big deal. Our refuge is in the stillness of being the compassionate witness to our panic and fear – not judging it as good or bad, just accepting the *what is* of the moment.

I feel anxious. Hmm, that's interesting. What's this about? What am I telling myself? What does it look like, feel like? Breathe. Feel your body. Does the anxiety have color, sound, texture, form? Where is it? Breathe, again, be with it. It's energy, just like a cloud, smoke, fire, or water. All your feelings, thoughts, and anxiety are just energy. Stay with it. Do Tonglin (see Chapter 31). Breathe into your frustration, breathe out clarity and light to your friend, to all people feeling frustrated in relationships.

If we remember that everything is our Buddha nature, we smile on ourselves, and remember we are now grown up. People will come and go. A new relationship may or may not work out, but we can walk the spiritual path – open, natural, and honest – and see what happens. If we realize that our ego creates soap operas to drown out the deeper dilemmas of existence, we can relax, be still, follow our breath and watch our melodrama from a distance. As our fears subside, we come out of our cocoon and once again notice the trees, delight in the smell of fresh laundry or children playing, and come back into remembering that we're part of all that is.

From this safe place, we can remove our masks, look in the mirror and accept this package of imperfections, fears, and blemishes. We remember, too, that our new friend is also a package deal – imperfect and beautiful – no more able to salve our hurts and fill our emptiness than the masks we just hung on the wall.

28

Notice the Flow of Giving
and Receiving

*The trees in your orchard . . . give that they may live, for
to withhold is to perish.*
> —KAHLIL GIBRAN, *The Prophet*

Giving and receiving help us enter the river of spirit
that connects us to each other. To give to others is to feel
the joy of creation spilling from us. To receive is to be
humbled, to shed our ego and allow another person to
penetrate our barriers. We let them know they matter
to us, they affect us. Our receptive heart becomes a
gift to the giver. When love pierces our hearts, tears may
rise because love flushes out anything that is buried.

Generosity says a great deal about a person's
emotional and spiritual development. When it's hard to
give, or it feels like ripping away a part of the self, we
are still anchored in our attachments or stories we've
created about scarcity. If this applies to you, make
friends with that part of you that feels resentful or finds
it difficult to give.

We can't force ourselves to give when we're not ready. Ken Keyes, who wrote *Handbook to Higher Consciousness*, gave sage advice when he said, 'Don't give a present you can't afford to give.' To explore this idea, examine your motivation with a finely tuned heart. If you are keeping score, feel resentful, or are giving in order to charm, seduce, entice, or impress someone, or make them feel indebted to you so you can ply them with guilt – don't do it. That isn't giving, it's the ego being a trickster.

True giving reveals an open heart, full and abundant. This feeling of abundance will happen naturally as you strip away the layers of your false self and live from your essence. Compassion and kindness will flow forth as well. As you immerse yourself in the spiritual journey you will stop clutching to things and shielding your heart.

I hasten to say, generosity of the heart is not measured by the number of presents or the cost of the bouquet. It's our generosity with our eyes, our listening, our kisses, our thoughtfulness . . . *and* the mementos we bring to our beloved.

The point of being aware of the flow of giving and receiving is to be mindful of the balance in a new relationship. While over time, giving and receiving fluctuate in relationships, in the beginning, if we want a spiritual equal, the energy must go in both directions. You can help the balance by pulling back a little if you are the one giving too much. If the other person comes forward, the flow between you will come into balance. If the other person doesn't come forward, well, that's information to consider. If it starts to feel as if you are toughing it out *not* to give, then, you may want to bring up your concerns. If the imbalance continues, you need to accept this as a truth about your relationship and decide if it's good for you.

Eventually, as we pass through love's door, giving and receiving merge into a continuous flow within the shared heart – like our breath coming in and going out. Different but not different. The same but not the same.

Part 4

KEEP LOYAL TO YOUR JOURNEY:
stay awake, stay aware

29

Make Friends with Your Fears

You are love itself – when you are not afraid.
—Sri Nisargadatta Maharaj, *I Am That*

It has often been suggested that there are two basic emotions – love and fear. When we feel love we are free of fear and when we feel fear we are unable to love. For most of us these moments come and go like thoughts and waves: fear and love, love and fear. From a Buddhist perspective, if we're not feeling love, we're confused or caught in an illusion.

We can be afraid someone *won't* love us, and we can be afraid that someone *will* love us. If someone *doesn't* want to be with us, we fear being alone and feeling defective. If someone *does* love us, we fear we won't measure up, they'll leave, or we'll get bored. If we're feeling disconnected from our center, we can fear just about anything.

Fear signals that we have bumped into our false core beliefs and forgotten the luminous essence within us. If we question the chain of assumptions we attach to fearful situations, we can often ease the intensity of our fear. I call it the 'then what' exercise. It might go like this:

'I'm afraid of getting involved, I might get left.'
'Then what (if you do get left)?'
'Well, I'd be alone.'
'Then what?'
'I'd be lonely.'
'Then what?'
'I'll scream and cry and be mad.'
'Then what?'
'I'll probably get tired and go to sleep.'
'Then what?'

As you read this, can you feel the intensity thin out? Often the mind goes blank, or it all starts to seem funny because we see our melodramatic thoughts as separate from our true essence.

Another way to approach feelings of fear is to pose the quantum question mentioned earlier: Without memory, mind or associations, what is fear? Again, our mind usually goes blank, because without memory, mind, or associations, we don't have strong reactions to anything. It all becomes energy.

On a more earthly level, we need to recognize that fear stems from the old familiar stories we've created to protect ourselves. But what is there to fear, really? As an adult no one can truly 'abandon' us unless we're falling off a cliff and they let go of our rope. People will either stay or leave, just as we will. *The only person who can reject us is ourself.*

Often when we have a gripping fear of losing someone, it's tied to a string of unresolved losses from the past. We fear we'll start crying and never be able to stop. But to find our heart we need to meet this reservoir of grief. We can use the 'then what' exercise to explore fears of sadness. It sometimes starts out as *I'll cry for two days, it will never stop,* and shifts to *My nose will get red, I'll get hungry, I'll have to go to the bathroom, and I'll probably get tired of crying.* If we follow any fearful thought to its logical conclusion we find that most of them thin out and lose their grip. They usually have their origin in a story we made up long ago – a story no longer relevant to us as an adult.

Some of us have been conditioned not to recognize fear. Here is a brief list of behavior that often overlays fear.

1. Blaming, attacking, being defensive.

2. Chattering, staying busy, being restless.

3. Boredom, anxiety, sleepiness.

4. Picking at people, being critical.

5. Making excuses.

6. Engaging in addictive or compulsive behavior.

7. Putting on a mask of any sort.

Another way to explore fear is through the following continuums. If at any given time you tune into these variables and note where you are, you will have a sense of your level of fear.

```
Love ................................... Fear
Connected ...................... Disconnected
Honest............................ Dishonest
Aware ........................ Unconscious
```

There is a fear-to-excitement ratio that shifts for most people as they become experienced at pushing their limits. Uusually the first time we try a new adventure, fear is high, excitement is low. But with repeated experiences of taking risks and feeling the joy of expanding our horizons, we approach adventure with a high level of excitement and a low level of fear. For most of us, the first day of school, the first piano recital, the first time on a bike, the first date, and the first kiss were all scary. But we did these things anyhow, and usually, with practice, we found they got easier.

The path from fear to love *is* the spiritual journey. When we tell the truth about ourselves, let go of compulsive behaviors, stop making excuses, we will naturally feel less fear and more love because we've removed the masks of fear. We don't create love, we simply let go of our false selves, and feel the love that has always been shining brightly at the core of our being.

30

Make Friends with Your Ambivalence

Where did I come from, and how?
Where am I going?
Will I know the road?

This life is empty breath.
If I can hear one clear truth,
I'll be fortunate.

—LULLA, *Naked Song*

Ambivalence is like having an internal argument that creates confusion: *I want to have a lover, I'm scared to have a lover; I want to feel close, I'm scared to feel close.* If you haven't found a partner after making a concerted effort, you might have some unexplored inner messages that say *I'm unworthy, I'm afraid of getting hurt again, I don't have anything to give, my career is my first priority, relationships are too hard*, and so on.

Your ambivalence might also contain some important clues to what you're really wanting in a relationship. Here's a way to explore your ambivalence.

...ample uses what Julia wrote (you
...in the chapter on writing personals ads).

...oring Ambivalence Exercise

STEP 1. _Write down all the things you appreciate about
single life._

Julia's example: I can go to sleep and get up when I
want. I can read myself to sleep. I have lots of energy
for my work. I can control the food that is in the
house so I'm not tempted. There aren't any argu-
ments or hassles. I have solitude when I want it. I can
play the piano when I want to. No one is jealous of
my friends.

STEP 2. _Write down all the fears you have about
becoming partnered with someone._

Julia's example: I'm afraid of giving more than I
should and getting depressed again. I'm afraid of sex
going dead. I'm afraid of losing attraction and desire.
I'm afraid of someone taking more than they give so I
become depleted. I'm afraid of someone being jealous
of my work. I'm afraid we won't get to a deep level of
intimacy and it will feel empty and I'll want to leave.
I'm afraid I'll like him and he'll want to leave.

STEP 3. _Write down all the reasons you want a relation-
ship._

Julia's example: I want to grow and expand, the way
a relationship pushes you to do – to make my love
bigger and more embracing. I want to feel special
to someone, to have companionship. I want to be
connected, to learn the meaning of love, sexuality,
and intimacy. I love planning a weekend with a lover,
taking trips, sharing new experiences, adventuring

together. I love the feeling of smiling across the table because we know just what the other is thinking, of cherishing each other's little weird behaviors and being able to laugh. It might work out, and even if it doesn't, I will learn and grow. It's nice being a couple. More people invite you over. You can be in a couples' group. I'd have someone to dance with, to kiss.

STEP 4. *Go back and read the three paragraphs you wrote.*

What is your immediate, uncensored reaction? Does one choice feel alive and clear, or are you pulled in several directions?

STEP 5. *Use your concerns, if any, to help you define what you want or signal when you need to become more secure in yourself.* For example, it was Julia's responsibility to work on her fear that she'd give more than she would receive. She could take control. Her fear of having a junk-food lover could be approached by looking for someone who would support her healthy eating habits.

As we take apart our ambivalence and see all the little pieces, we start to know ourselves more deeply, define ourselves more clearly, and thus become free to melt into the heart of another.

31

Practice Tonglin:
a meditation for healing and compassion

Develop the good heart, that longs for other beings to find lasting happiness, and acts to secure that happiness.
> —SOGYAL RINPOCHE,
> *The Tibetan Book of Living and Dying*

There is no need for temples: no need for complicated philosophy.
Our own brain, our own heart is our temple . . .
> —THE DALAI LAMA

Tonglin is a form of meditation that helps us transform feelings of anger, fear, hurt, and sadness in ourselves and others. It helps us relax into our own pain and be present to the pain of others.

An example of the spirit of Tonglin occurred at a recent meeting of mental health professionals. Tensions were high, an argument erupted, and the hostility in the room was palpable. Then Al, a participant, stood up, looked around the room and said, with a droll smile, 'I sure feel a whole lot of love in here.' Everyone laughed and the tensions eased. Tonglin works like that; it cuts the tension and brings light into dense situations.

Tonglin asks that we breathe in the suffering, negativity, and pain of others and then breathe out calmness, clarity, and joy. When I first read about Tonglin in the Tibetan Book of Living and Dying – 'imagine that all of his or her sufferings manifest together and gather into a great mass of hot, black, grimy smoke' – I couldn't fathom wanting to breathe that in. I was afraid that smoke would get stuck and I'd get sick.

Later, when I read a description of Tonglin in Pema Chodron's books, I was less resistant, and since then it has become part of my daily practice. I now see it more like Al's remark – a way to cut through tension and anxiety.

Tonglin is the opposite of many approaches to dealing with pain and discomfort, which encourage you to breathe in light and love and breathe out your anger, hurt, or pain. From a Buddhist perspective, breathing out anger, hurt, and pain is like sending toxins to the universe, an unfriendly and separating thing to do.

Instead of turning our heads from pain, we merge with it, neither holding onto it nor pushing it away, becoming instead an instrument of transformation. Recently, on my early morning drive to the health club, I saw a deer in the middle lane, trying to get up, but obviously crippled. Her eyes looked confused and frightened. As I drove by I breathed in her pain and breathed out a blessing. I could feel a dark cloud swirling inside of me, but I also had an image of a deer running freely in the woods. I can never know if it helped her, but something loosened up inside of me. Instead of turning from her pain, I joined her. It was then I realized more deeply the power of Tonglin.

PREPARATION FOR TONGLIN MEDITATION

Here are three possible ways to prepare yourself for Tonglin.

1. Drop down into a quiet place, let go of mind, memories, and associations, and feel the stillness that results.
2. Breathe into the area around your heart and imagine it softening. Imagine your heart center becoming light, spacious, and free.
3. Bring up a memory when someone was especially loving and kind to you, or a time when you felt great love in your heart.

The following are some ways to practice Tonglin. You can do just one, or do them in sequence. They expand from focusing on oneself to connecting with all people. If all these instructions seem like a lot to take on, simply do one step: When you feel hurt, confused, lonely, or sad, breathe into your pain, feel it, be with it, then breathe out an image of clarity, light, and a blessing. This alone will start to change your life.

TONGLIN FOR YOURSELF

When you feel hurt, frustrated, upset and so on, breathe into the feeling, let the energy swirl around, and send out care, love, and a blessing for yourself and your pain.

When you breathe in you might even notice the color, texture, edges, or shape of your feelings. When you breathe out, you can imagine a stream of light.

TONGLIN FOR YOURSELF AND SOMEONE YOU KNOW

On the in breath, feel your heartache or frustration with someone, and on the out breath send out love, clarity, and compassion to both of you.

TONGLIN FOR ANOTHER PERSON

On the in breath, feel the pain of someone you know. Take it in, feel it inside. Then send out light, calm, and a blessing to that person. (I do this frequently during psychotherapy sessions.)

TONGLIN FOR ALL PEOPLE

On the in breath, feel your pain and then the pain of all people who have similar frustrations and conflicts. On the out breath, send light, loving energy with a blessing to all people in conflict.

SHARE YOUR HAPPINESS WITH EVERYONE

The next time you feel joy and delight while walking in a park, hearing the birds, listening to music, or enjoying a close moment with a friend, breathe in your happiness and send it to everyone.

32

Tonglin Meditation for Couples

As a psychotherapist, I have started using Tonglin with couples. Many people get lost in words and find solace in connecting through the breath in an intentional silence. They also become able to access a deeper level of awareness. Anyone can do this with a partner or friend.

Sit facing each other, relax, and entrain your breathing to each other. Breathe in and out until you feel the synchronized rhythm. You may instinctively want to close your eyes, which is all right, but after a while it can be helpful to make soft eye contact. (Gently attune to the presence of the other and make eye contact without staring deeply into each other's eyes.)

- If one person is having difficulty, both of you can breathe in that person's fear or pain, and breathe out healing clarity and compassion.
- If there is a conflict between the two of you, name the conflict, and each of you breathe it in, feel it completely, and send out a blessing to your partner and to the relationship.

(Sometimes our ego has a fit at the very thought of sending light energy to someone who's been hurtful, let alone look them in the eyes. But if you can gently step over the ego and try it, you might be amazed. If nothing else, it intervenes on old patterns and gives you a new way to be together.)

- If as a couple you are seeking guidance, take some time to name the conflict, then synchronize your breathing again. Breathe in the confusion and send out clarity and light to 'the relationship.' (You might do this on a daily basis when trying to bridge an impasse or make an important decision.)
- Another step is for the couple to imagine breathing in the pain of all couples feeling conflict and breathing out a blessing. This has a transforming effect on the mind because it transports us to the realm of 'big mind,' or the universal heart. Instead of feeling caught in your isolated problems, you will move into connection with all people sharing similar difficulties, and realize you are simply sitting together feeling *the* hurt, *the* frustration, and *the* sadness that are intrinsic to human relationships. After a while you will no longer feel alone, and little daily problems will loosen their grip on your ego so you can meet them with grace and a light heart.

33

What to Do When You Want to Run

When you've been hoping for a lover and relishing the possibility of having a committed companion, it can be upsetting when instead of welcoming a new love, you feel an urge to run away. If you listen for the answer, you might hear a distant voice inside crying, *I'll be caught, trapped, smothered*, or perhaps, *You can't love me, I don't deserve it*. These stories reflect a wounded part of yourself that needs your compassion and love.

When you feel the urge to run, you have two choices: 1) Blame the other person. Pick at him or her, and build up your case that something is wrong with him or her. Leave and repeat the pattern with someone else. Or, 2) Sit down and suffer your terror, talk with your self, stay put and breathe. Tell yourself you can stand the discomfort. It's not dangerous. Your willingness to explore what lies beneath the urge to run can free you to love.

For some people, the challenge is to receive love. When Amy first met Ellie, she felt blessed beyond measure. As Ellie continued to show affection and care, Amy felt torn between a desire to push her away and a longing to be together. She realized the conflict was internal and fuelled by the core belief 'I'll always be left alone' that stemmed from her mother's death when she was five. With psychotherapy and body work, she was able to start making friends with this belief and the layers of grief that had encased her heart. Gradually, she came to believe that love doesn't always mean someone will leave. And even if Ellie left, she realized that, as an adult, she could handle it. This eventually freed her to open her heart to Ellie.

Anne and Jerry were committed to their marriage, but they ran away from each other emotionally. It was a second marriage for both, and each of them was dealing with a legacy of trauma, hers from childhood abuse and his from his experiences in Vietnam. When they tried to talk about problems they'd speak in therapy jargon, or be overly polite for fear of upsetting the other. Because they were both willing to journey inward and face their terror, they were able to surmount the overwhelming odds against them.

In a counseling session, I asked them to stand apart, facing each other, at whatever distance was completely comfortable. They stood about six feet apart. I gave them a ten-foot rope to hold onto, signifying the distance between them as well as their bond to each other.

'I want you to be completely honest with each other as you take turns talking about the relationship,' I said. 'If your response is to move back on the rope, do so, if it's to move closer, do that.' I then suggested they take turns talking about the relationship. At first, they spoke stiffly, using generalizations to distance themselves from their feelings – 'I think there's a lot of control in *the* relationship,' Anne said. Every time one of them raised a question or a disagreement, the other would step away. It was like a deeply conditioned fight or flight response.

After a while, I suggested they talk in pithy language a ten-year-old would understand – 'I like it when you . . . I hate it when you . . . I get scared when you . . .' Instead of stepping back, I asked them to remain where they were and see what happened. I wanted them to experience that conflict is not mortally dangerous. Suddenly, when Jerry took a big step closer to Anne, fear flashed across her face.

'What's happening, Anne?' I asked.

Tears erupted and Anne's words tumbled out. 'I can't really believe you want to be with me. I'm always so afraid you'll leave.'

Jerry looked paralyzed.

'What are you feeling?' I asked Jerry.

'I feel terrible, as if I've done something wrong.'

'What did you hear Anne say?' I asked.

'I don't know, but I feel guilty, as if I should be able to take her pain away.'

'Tell her that,' I said to him.

'I feel like I should be able to stop your pain.'

'Just be here,' Anne said, moving closer.

Jerry's eyes welled up with tears. 'I can't believe you want to be with me either. I have such a hard time talking. I'm so scared. I feel so inadequate.'

Anne and Jerry kept talking, stepping into fear, feeling it shake their inner world. They hung onto the rope – their bond, their commitment. Eventually, their voices relaxed and became more natural as they became acclimated to staying close during an emotionally charged exchange.

'I appreciate you so much, Jerry,' Anne said suddenly. Jerry froze.

After a long pause I said, 'Jerry, can you step closer and feel in your heart what she is saying?' As he stepped forward and she reached out a hand to him, his breath tightened. Then, in a surprising simultaneous moment, both stepped forward and laughter erupted as they collapsed into an embrace. They had made it through a force field, stepped over land mines to reveal their hearts, and taken the first step toward not running away.

I am filled by the light of a thousand angels
Softening my way, softening my way
I am filled by the light of a thousand angels,
softening my way to you.

I am washed by the tears of a thousand angels
Softening my way, softening my way
I am washed by the tears of a thousand rainbows,
softening my way to you.
                    —A Dance of Universal Peace

To come together instead of running away, we must journey through our fears, softening our hearts and making room for each other, remembering that we are already filled with the light of a thousand angels, with spirit and pure love. We need to grab hold of our bond, stay connected and reveal our true feelings, instead of hiding and running away. Sometimes this includes turning off the TV, stopping all use of alcohol, and taking a break from working long hours, having an immaculate home, or being eternally busy. Just stop. Look at each other. Listen in the silence.

An open heart creates a shelter for ourselves and for our relationship. It helps bridge our separateness and allows us to discover the amazing blessing of an intimate bond. Creating this is not easy, but I don't know of any couple that regrets the journey.

34

Be a Spiritual Warrior:
set a bottom line

*Awareness, courage, and gentleness are the basic
'weapons' of the warrior of the heart.*

—John Welwood

Because we want to find the luminous essence within
us, because we do not want to repeat painful lessons of
the past, because we love ourselves fiercely and want
to find a partner who is kind and loving, we commit to
what is often called a bottom line. Setting a bottom line
means naming the behaviors you will not tolerate in a
relationship. Period. Nonnegotiable. If someone crosses
the bottom line we stop seeing them – no rationalizing,
no excuses. Likewise, we set a bottom line for our
own behavior – making excuses for the other person,
ignoring responsibilities, sacrificing our values to keep
the other person. Honoring our bottom line tests our
spiritual resolve. It's incredibly easy to forget when our
hormones or longing get involved but that's why we
have brains and, I would add, feet.

To set a bottom line, think back on a past troubled relationship. Remember the first inklings you had of something amiss. Remember that uneasiness gnawing in your gut, the tight chest, the worry, the confusion, the loss of energy. Remember the rationalizations and excuses you made as you tried to ignore behavior that finally became unbearable. When I've tracked back with myself and my clients in unhealthy relationships, we *always* find there were numerous red flags early on that were ignored or rationalized, often starting with the first date.

MAXIM
Past behavior is the best predictor of future behavior.

SUGGESTION
Trust your observations and intuitive responses.
Bring up your concerns as they appear.

You can use these four lists to help set your own bottom line:

1. Red flag behavior on the other person.
2. Red flag behavior of your own.
3. Rationalizations and stories you've used to disregard your bottom line in the past.
4. Consequences of disregarding your bottom line or not taking care of yourself.

Here are some samples drawn from several people's bottom-line lists.

LIST #1. RED FLAG BEHAVIOR OF THE OTHER PERSON (Remember the Warning Signs You Ignored in Past Relationships That Signaled Trouble.)

- Is superficially charming. Seduces you emotionally and physically in order to have control. Wants immediate sex and commitment. Seems too good to be true.
- Does not respect limits or boundaries. Ignores you when you say no.
- Has a volatile temper, explodes over small things.
- Is jealous of your friends, work, and other interests – always wants to know where you are. Makes snide remarks about your friends.
- Constantly breaks dates and agreements (being stood up one time without a genuine apology is sufficient reason to stop seeing someone.)
- Is unreliable. Says s/he'll call and then 'forgets.' Constantly makes excuses.
- Doesn't show genuine interest in being together.
- Chronically blames others. Never sees his/her part in creating problems, which are always about you, others, the weather, their childhood, their past spouse or lover, etc.
- Is deeply enmeshed with mother, father, children, or past lover – either dependent or very angry.
- Refuses to introduce you to his/her friends – keeps you separated from the rest of his or her life.
- Parades you around like a trophy.
- Becomes violent, verbally or physically.
- Never has any money, expects you to pay for everything, doesn't give back.
- Has active addictions: drugs, alcohol, gambling, anorexia, bulimia, etc.

- Is extremely out of control with money and work.

LIST #2. RED FLAG BEHAVIOR OF YOUR OWN

Items on the following list signal that we need to get to work on ourselves. *Remember, it's better to speak up and let a relationship fall apart than to live in fear, or sacrifice your integrity.*

Here are signs of losing your self and your power in a relationship.

- Not bringing up concerns and problems for fear of conflict or 'hurting' or 'threatening' the other person.
- Feeling like a little child around the other person.
- Feeling confused, hazy, mushy, afraid, dreamy, disconnected.
- Acting cute, charming, tough, super competent, cheerful, sweet, cool, seductive, as a woeful victim, and so on.
- Molding your life around their needs – ceasing to see your own friends, giving up hobbies, and so on.
- Giving a lot more than comes back, or wanting to take but not give.
- Feelings of desperation, neediness, wanting to cling to the person.
- Jumping into future fantasies – wedding, living together, etc.
- Giving lots of advice or trying to change the other person.
- Rationalizing, ignoring, or making excuses about troublesome behavior.
- Hoping the other person will change – if you are only nice enough, sexy enough, good enough, generous enough, or love them enough.
- Obsessing about the other person.
- Increasing indulgence in addictive or compulsive behaviors – eating, shopping, drinking, gambling, etc.

- Being sexual against your wishes or when you know it isn't a good idea.
- Wanting lots of sex to prove you have a relationship or are loved.
- Not taking care of yourself or being responsible – staying up too late, not eating well, not exercising, not paying bills, and so on.

LIST #3. RATIONALIZATIONS AND STORIES YOU'VE USED TO DISREGARD YOUR BOTTOM LINE IN THE PAST

We often make up lots of stories to avoid hearing when our gut signals that trouble is brewing. Here is a sample list of common stories/rationalizations used to mask our fear and avoid reality.

'Nobody's perfect.'

'I know s/he really loves me, s/he just has a hard time expressing it.'

'He means well, he just loses control sometimes.'

'If I complain s/he'll go away.'

'He's just going through a hard time.'

'I made a commitment.'

'S/he needs me.'

'I know there are problems but God sent him/her to me.'

'We're soul mates.'

'Other people have it worse.'

'I might never meet anyone else.'

LIST #4. CONSEQUENCES OF DISREGARDING YOUR BOTTOM LINE OR NOT TAKING CARE OF YOURSELF

Scan your past relationships for the following symptoms. Write down the names of people you've been with in the past and make a list for each one. Here are some ideas to get you started.

- Wasted a lot of time and energy.
- Became dependent, needy, afraid of being alone.
- Took the focus off my goals, work, integrity, values.
- Got depressed, anxious, lost my creativity.
- Got irritable, critical, controlling, mean toward the other person.
- Engaged in addictions and compulsive behavior involving food, drugs, alcohol, shopping, codependency, etc.
- Didn't see other friends, or repeatedly burdened them with my troubles.
- Had physical symptoms of stress – sleeplessness, headaches, stomachaches, and so on.
- Felt a seething rage inside.
- Felt stuck in my life.

VERY IMPORTANT MESSAGE!
IF YOU ARE SERIOUS ABOUT NOT REPEATING THE DRAMAS OF THE PAST:
1. Post your bottom line on your fridge. Put a check mark by any item on your bottom line that gets disregarded or rationalized away. Do it every time it happens.
2. Give copies of your bottom-line list to one or two friends, or people in a support group. Report to them regularly on how you are doing and ask them to remind you when you disregard your bottom line or start rationalizing.

Most friends will be relieved to have permission to speak up when you are engaging in destructive behavior. If people don't feel free to be honest with you, they are likely to withdraw from the friendship to avoid hearing your predictable tales of misery. Or they might do the opposite, they'll join you in blaming the other person and reinforce that you are the innocent victim, which will compound your dramatic misery. By the way, one teaching of Buddhism is that we help our friends grow, we don't collude with their desperate and crazy behavior. We help them stay on the path.

When your bottom line starts looking like a crossed-off grocery list, call forth your inner warrior and have a conversation. *Okay, how am I conning myself? How am I making this other person more important than my own life? What would I want to say to a friend who was acting the way I am?* We need to remember our path, our spirit, and our sanity and protect ourselves. Get help. No partner is worth scrambling your brains.

Sticking to our bottom line tests our mettle and will. It can feel like waging an inner war, but along with feelings of withdrawal – loneliness, fear, guilt, and emptiness – we feel a new kind of freedom when we remain loyal to ourselves.

Only when we have a warrior within – aware, kind, self-protective, fierce, able to say no – do we have the security to shed our protective skin and say yes to another. Our sentinel is our guardian, the wise one who protects us. Our warrior is also the cousin of tenderness, kindness, and compassion because it releases fear and allows us to become vulnerable. Our warrior is attuned to the rhythm, tone, pulse, harmony, and dissonance of the relationship and open to unsparing self-examination. He or she is able to bring up conflict and concerns, and walk away from a harmful situation, no matter how alluring or tempting the pull.

35

What's That Buzzing in My Brain?:
handling obsessions

Someone who doesn't make flowers makes thorns.
If you're not building rooms where wisdom
can be openly spoken, you're building a prison.
                              —RUMI, from *Say I Am You*

In the first weeks or months of dating someone who shows promise, anxious thoughts may float through our mind: *Does she really like me? Will he stay? Is this for real?* A certain amount of uneasiness is natural because it's too soon to know what the outcome of the relationship will be. If we start obsessing to the point where it feels like a nonstop buzz in the brain, however, we're probably hiding from the truth and not voicing our feelings, fears, or concerns to ourself or our new friend.

Obsessive thinking signals that we are not telling the truth either to ourself or another person.

Obsessive thinking can feel like one's brain is invaded from morning until night. No matter how you try, it just keeps buzzing. Sometimes you constantly replay conversations – either real or imagined, have euphoric recall of a past sexual experience, or feel as if their name or face won't stop flashing in your brain.

An obsession can signal:

1. A need to bring up hurts or concerns.
2. The intuitive knowledge that your new love is ambivalent, can't commit, or is keeping secrets from you.
3. A need to ask for clarification of the intentions of your new 'friend.' (What is the status of our relationship?)
4. You are addicted to romance and creating the illusion of a relationship which has nothing to do with reality.
5. You aren't admitting to yourself that you have serious doubts about being with this person. You want to want to be with him or her, but something doesn't feel right.

Over and over, in my life and in working with clients, I have observed that when people let themselves know the truth, and speak the truth, the obsessing goes away and the mind quiets down. Knowing and acknowledging the truth is not easy, partly because the signals may be nonverbal – a chronic queasiness in our stomach, a loss of energy, feeling hazy, overeating, or a lump in the throat.

Our task is to fearlessly, and with great compassion, listen to what our body, mind, and heart are saying and remember that obsessive thinking keeps us locked in fear. If you're caught in fear, call forth your adult self to remind you that you managed your life before you met this person, and you are *not* dependent on him or her. You can get out of bed, dress yourself, feed yourself, go to work, and take yourself to the movies. It's an illusion to believe that you *need* him or her so desperately, an echo from childhood.

  A phrase to repeat over and over again: I will not live in fear.

Better to have a fight, stir it all up, have the relationship fall apart, and be on your own than to live with a chronic tight chest and clutter in your brain. Sometimes there is no need to speak to the other person; rather, you need to realize you are caught in an illusion. You're making up a story that is a thousand miles from reality. Other times you need to bring up concerns.

Almost magically, when we voice our truths an obsession will fade. It might mean you have an argument or end the relationship. But it might also mean that you have a productive conversation, get clarity about your commitment, feel closer and take a big step toward a rich authentic partnership. Certainly, you will increase your self-respect and stay steady on the spiritual path supported by clarity, truth, and taking good care of yourself.

36

Set Your Attraction Radar to Find a Loving Partner

Sometimes our attraction radar goes repeatedly in the wrong direction. People who are kind, caring, and good leave us indifferent and bored, while hot, dazzling, irresponsible charmers spark our interest. If you are attracted to people who are not good for you, list their attributes and learn to say to yourself, 'Even though I'm attracted to this person, I know it won't work,' and walk the other way. This doesn't mean you will instantly find a great partner, but you will create a spaciousness in your life so you can better reflect on the false beliefs that compel you to be attracted to someone who is unable to join you on the spiritual path.

I went through a period where I was drawn toward charming, intelligent, liberal, passive-aggressive, and (sometimes) alcoholic men who were emotionally withholding and unable to commit. Their facile words were not reflected in their behavior. Finally, I'd had enough painful lessons and said, 'That's enough. No more.' The very act of walking away helped me have more self-respect and eventually led to internal change.

I eventually figured out that my attraction to people who held an emotional carrot in front of me, and repeatedly snatched it away, was a replay of my relationship with my mother. Unconsciously, I still wanted to get her love so I was picking out people who were emotionally withholding (like she was) and hoping they'd change (as she didn't). The story I had made up about myself that kept this pattern in place was that I would always be alone.

While I couldn't instantly erase the thoughts, I could start observing them and realizing they were just thoughts. I didn't fight them, but I didn't dwell on them either. Eventually, with both counseling and meditation, the thoughts thinned out and became less intense, like soft clouds.

One woman who went from a painful relationship to a loving one said that she simply resolved that she would only be with someone who was good to her. The man she met, and eventually married, did not dazzle her at first, and she had to remind herself to stay present and be aware of her feelings. 'I felt relaxed and unworried, almost as if something were wrong. My old experience with relationships was tension and excitement. He was dependable and tender, which I ultimately came to treasure.'

Notice how she changed her story about what signalled a good relationship. As we continue on the path of becoming less attached to our stories we stop believing them, stop telling them, and start going deeper inside to our luminous center, which will naturally be attracted to a loving, compassionate person who can give and receive love.

37

Is It Written in the Stars –
or on a Page?:
astrology and graphology

Sometimes we're unsure of our perceptions in a relationship. We're troubled but don't know quite why. Other times we start being irritated with the other person for no obvious reason. While we should never stop listening to our inner guidance, handwriting analysis and astrology can sometimes give us insight or validate our hunches.

In my own experience, both have proven helpful in better understanding a partner, validating my reality, and realizing that we all have different ways of being in the world – from learning styles, to our rhythm in forming a relationship, to different ways of perceiving the world. As an example, in talking with Jane Yank of Signature Consulting (see Resources) about a relationship, she said, 'Charlotte, for you talking things over is like breathing air, for him it's like doing push-ups.' This one comment helped me be far more tender toward the man I was dating and appreciate what a big effort it was for him to talk with me.

HANDWRITING ANALYSIS

Jane, a certified graphologist, spoke of the possible uses of handwriting analysis for new couples or people who are dating.

'The basic thesis is that we're highly socialized in this culture. There are courses in how to present yourself, how to flirt, how to say the "right" thing. So we get prepackaged people. Without a yenta [a Yiddish term for a very savvy woman who was often hired as a matchmaker] who has known us since we were a child, we have little to go on except gut instinct and the presentation someone is making to us.

'Handwriting gives an inside look into who people really are. It's a composite of all that's in their past. It shows people's interests, talents, intellectual capacity, ways of thinking, energy level, degree of openness, and typical ways of reacting to stress. You can even uncover old emotional injuries that were life-shaping events that someone might have carefully covered by the right appearance, and the right lingo.

'In exploring compatibility, we know there will be differences, but the question to ask is, *what meaning do the differences have?* Can they be understood and accepted or do they signal some basic problems that will permeate a relationship?

'For example, energy level affects compatibility because it relates to the ability to follow through on plans and goals and the depth of commitment that person is able to make. Some people may very much want a relationship, but simply do not have the emotional or physical capacity to sustain it – they are always shifting internally and don't feel clear about who they are.'

Handwriting analysis gives people a quick way to recognize self-deception. According to Jane, 'Some people who wish to be a certain way convince themselves of their desired persona, and then misrepresent themselves. Others use charm and manipulation to shield a demanding approach to life. It may take months of dating before you can see through the façade, although you might start having uneasy feelings long before you recognize the deception. With a handwriting analysis, you will have an indication right away. You can also see how people handle stress. It ranges from coping skillfully to becoming defensive or withdrawn to having a propensity toward aggression.'

I asked Jane about gender differences in handwriting. She laughed. 'Handwriting is definitely an equal opportunity measure. It's hard to tell between male or female handwriting, and there are tremendous individual differences between all people. It clearly shows that we need to confront our stereotypes and stop making assumptions about what a man is like or what a woman is like. Everyone has their own constellation of attributes which are unique.'

Jane went on to say that she often works with couples who have hit a roadblock to help them better understand each other. I asked her if she felt it was ethical for one person in a relationship to ask for a handwriting analysis of a partner or someone he or she is just dating, without asking the other's permission. She said that while it obviously reflects a lack of trust, and she prefers people to come in together, she could see times when it could be extremely useful. For example, when someone is in an abusive situation and having trouble believing their perceptions, handwriting analysis can help that person see that their partner has a deeply ingrained pattern of dealing with stress through hostility and aggression. Also, people might come in alone when they are older or have been burned before and don't want to waste their time pursuing a relationship when they have little chance of being compatible with their potential partner.

Graphologists use very refined instruments to measure details of handwriting, and their analysis is based on massive research. Jane said that she checks three measurements for any attribute to see if it is consistent in the handwriting. Even so, she always poses her interpretations to clients as questions: 'Does this feel right to you?'

ASTROLOGY

Part of me finds it hard to believe that the time and place of my birth is central to making predictions about my temperament, relationships, personality, and so on. Stephen Wolinsky described astrology as giving us a snapshot of the space-time relationship when we were born, as well as other events in our lives. 'If the moon can pull the oceans, and we are ninety-five percent liquid, the positioning of the stars and the moon would seem to have an effect on our bodies.' While I don't pretend to truly understand why it works, the several astrological readings I have had in the past, including two compatibility charts, have been extraordinarily accurate in helping me understand both myself and a potential partner in a relationship.

I met with Altazar Player, an experienced astrologer, for an interview and to have him do a compatibility chart for me and a person I was seeing. According to Altazar, astrology charts can predict numerous aspects of compatibility – trust, common interests, and the ability to connect, be understood, communicate, and generally match each other's energy. He also had said that dating services that used astrology to predict compatibility raised their success rates in matching people as a result. Along with providing compatibility charts to help people look at the strengths and problems of a given relationship, Altazar has designed an 'Ideal Mate Profile' that provides the specific years, dates, and months of the birthdate of a person's most appropriate partner. As with couples or individuals wanting hand-writing analysis, Altazar often does compatibility charts early in a new relationship.

'The idea isn't to say, "Okay, this is a bad compatibility chart, you should break up." The purpose is to help the couple be more conscious of areas of difficulty and be more understanding of each other. Although sometimes,' he added, 'the compatibility looks bleak or it's clear that people would make better friends than lovers.'

If you are uneasy about choosing a partner, have doubts you want to validate, want to understand yourself and your partner better, or want to try handwriting analysis or astrology just for the sake of curiosity, these two methods can be of use. Be sure to ask the astrologer or graphologist about their experience, training, and belief system. And remember, never override your own common sense, observation, and intuition. On the spiritual path, we are open to information and guidance, but ultimately our internal wisdom is our guide.

38

Accept Impermanence, Loss, and Joy

Your joy is your sorrow unmasked . . .

The deeper that sorrow carves into your being, the more joy you can contain.

When you are joyous, look deep into your heart and you shall find it is only that which has given you sorrow that is giving you joy.

When you are sorrowful look again in your heart, and you shall see that in truth you are weeping for that which has been your delight.

—KAHLIL GIBRAN, *The Prophet*

To open ourselves to the joy of a loving union means accepting the possibility of loss. To be able to love, we need to accept the melancholy of life, the little losses of every day and the great loss called death. Paradoxically, once we accept that change, loss, discomfort, and grief are inevitable, life is not so frightening and we are freer to create intimate relationships.

We need to open ourselves to the inevitable daily losses of living, so we can open ourselves to love. We say hello and good-bye. We feel connected one moment and disconnected the next. A tender sexual moment will never be exactly the same. Every breath we take connects us to life, then passes, before a new breath fills us. We move through new developmental and spiritual stages daily, weekly.

Impermanence is a central concept in Buddhism. Nothing stays the same, not ideas, thoughts, perception, and certainly not other people. The flowers on the dining table will wilt in a few days, the clouds will never be the same again. Sadness and joy exist side by side. On the spiritual path we allow these things to be, observing them and watching them pass, just like a breeze. Don't expect the person you fall in love with to stay the same. Like breathing air, the spiritual path is fluid, ungraspable, undefinable, elusive. We stop the flow the moment we try to hold onto anything.

On a recent morning, I took a beautiful walk up Blue Mountain. The meadowlarks were singing, a gentle, clear, crisp breeze blew gently over my face, the sky shone blue against the huge ponderosa pines, and the path was soft with pine needles. I felt the pleasure of exertion as I walked uphill and felt my heart beating faster. As I reveled in the sensuous pleasure, I wanted to drink it up and take it home with me. But the moment I thought of hanging onto it, I could feel a tinge of sadness. I was no longer in the present. So I tuned into my feet on the trail and the beat of my heart and again savored the delectable moment.

You partner with someone as they are this moment. The vitality can remain if you adventure forth, side by side, savoring the moment to moment shifts and changes that inevitably arise as you both stay open to the journey. We need to look at each other anew every day, with clear eyes and an open mind so we see the person of today, not an image from the past.

We wanderers, ever seeking the lonelier way, begin no day where we have ended another day; and no sunrise finds us where sunset left us.
—KAHLIL GIBRAN, *The Prophet*

Part 5

GOING DEEPER:
create a durable fire

39

Going Deeper:
finding love beneath illusions

*There is the material world and the spiritual. Between lies
the universal mind which is also the universal heart. It is
wise love that makes the two one.*
—Sri Nisargadatta Maharaj, *I Am That*

As our connection deepens, we may feel the uneasiness
of walking a fragile line between fear, hope, and commitment. We don't know each other well enough to
make a long-term commitment, but our hopes start
rising. We dance between our desire to protect our
tender self and our desire to remain open enough to
help the relationship move forward.

Living with ambiguity is an enormous challenge for
many. Our expectations about how a relationship *should*
be sometimes block our ability to see what is truly
unfolding. It helps to stand back and observe the process. As we come to live more from essence and start to
believe it's natural to love, it's safe to be honest, and we
are in the heart of the Beloved no matter what, our

illusions slip away and we open ourselves to a deeper connection.

On the spiritual path we remember and we forget, we like and dislike, we are excited and disappointed. If we've put a halo on our beloved's head, we'll feel let down when it starts to tarnish. We feel a rude shock when our prince or princess gets enraged in traffic, criticizes what we're wearing, has bad breath, pouts when we go to see a friend, doesn't call for several days, or starts being moody. We need to remember this is the stuff of new relationships and a challenge to our spiritual path.

If our vision has stayed relatively clear and we aren't expecting perfection, we will be more bemused than disappointed by the flaws and foibles of our new love. Even so, we will often be faced with a fundamental question: Do the things that bother us reflect our illusions and need for control, or are they clear signs of trouble brewing in the relationship?

Even as (love) ascends to your height
and caresses your tenderest branches that quiver in the
  sun,
So shall love descend to your roots
and shake them in their clinging to the earth.
—KAHLIL GIBRAN, *The Prophet*

Allowing yourself to be shaken to your roots is a source of a growing relationship. We reach between our illusions and realize it's safe to talk about our feelings, it's safe to make requests, it's safe to sometimes say no. And most of all, it's safe to say yes. This doesn't guarantee the success of the relationship but it keeps us securely on the spiritual path. When we hear our inner dialogues, we remember we're listening to two parts of our personality having a tug of war. One voice inside says, *That's petty, don't bring it up, it might upset him (or her)*, while another voice says, *My gut aches, I need to talk about this now.* Once again, our ego and illusions are pitted against our desire to live from essence. We observe and remember:

> *There is nothing to fear in being guided by the truth. The ingredients for a relationship are either there or they aren't, and the truth helps you find out as soon as possible.*

Yet discerning our truths is not easy. It requires disciplined attention to our thoughts and feelings. Sometimes our truths come in spontaneous flashes of clarity. Other times, we need to look beyond the ruminations of our minds – the fleeting desires, opinions, and criticisms that seem momentarily real – and await a clear message from a deep inner stillness. It may take days, weeks, or even months. The art of living by our truths requires us to ask the questions: 'Is my motivation grounded in compassion? *When* do I say something? *How* do I say it? *Should* I say anything?' Some truths are conveyed by a warm glance, a touch, pulling away, coming together, waiting, silence. And we need to remember that what we call *the* truth is simply *our* truth at any given moment in time.

It may help to remember that we are not alone in our struggle to perceive our truths – we are exploring *the* fears, *the* conflicts, *the* struggles of *all* relationships. As we delve into revealing ourselves to each other, we are connecting with common human experiences. All authentic relationships include conflict and the challenge of staying awake. So if the dance of new love makes you feel jittery, well, just breathe and keep dancing. Remember, you live in the heart of the Beloved. You may not realize it or feel it, but underlying all your thoughts is your bright shining essence.

To keep from getting caught in illusions we can ground ourselves with some simple questions that help us reflect on the relationship.

- Are we both showing genuine interest in being together – does each person initiate contact and feel delight in creating a bond?
- Are we both keeping agreements – keeping dates, being on time, following through on promises?
- Do we both listen to each other and show respect and consideration?
- Are we sharing a wide range of experiences?
- Are we asking questions so we learn about each other's history, belief system, and values?
- Am I staying aware of my reactions, observations, and intuition?
- Am I noticing my feelings, doubts, and concerns, and bringing them up or exploring them within myself?
- What's the role of alcohol and other drugs in the picture? Do we drink (or use drugs) to help us talk openly or make love?

If I hold you with my emotions,
you'll become a wished-for companion.

If I hold you with my eyes,
you'll grow old and die.

So I hold you where we
both mix with the infinite.

—RUMI, from *Say I Am You*

40

The Sacred Circle of Beginnings and Endings

You moan, 'But she left me. He left me.'
Twenty more will come.
Be empty of worrying.
Think of Who Created Thought!

Why do you stay in prison
when the door is so wide open?
Move outside the tangle of fear-thinking
Live in Silence.
Flow down and down in always
widening rings of Being

—RUMI

In my late twenties, I left a painful marriage. I had been depressed and exhausted, and felt no hope that expending more energy would make the marriage work. Ironically, the parting with my husband was, perhaps, the sweetest part of our relationship. The common threads that had brought us together, the care we had once felt for each other, re-emerged, creating a strong desire not to cause suffering for each other. And because we didn't slam the door, ten years later, when I was going through therapy, I was able to call him and talk over some painful events from our marriage. He was right there with me, vulnerable and honest. The healing continued, the forgiveness became complete.

In the journey toward finding your beloved, there may be several endings and new beginnings. They are part of the same circle. The grace we bring to leaving a relationship will help us gently untie the cord and let go. Forgiving ourselves and our former partner frees us to love more wisely the next time. And if forgiveness seems impossible, imagine letting go of your resentments and hurt. If that doesn't feel possible, explore all your feelings of anger, grief, and hurt so they can be felt, understood, and released.

If you continue to feel bitter, wronged, or victimized, you need to explore the stories you are telling yourself. You might ask, 'What was my part in creating this story? How can I avoid making the same mistakes again?' As an adult we say to ouselves, *I chose this person, I loved this person, I stayed with this person, and now, what does it all mean about me?* Only when we have completed the process of letting go can we move on with clarity and openness to a new person. Otherwise, we will be protecting our wounded heart, loving half-heartedly, and feeling disappointment because we never seem to get truly close to anyone.

No parting should ever come as a surprise. If instead of holding back and building up grudges or resentments, we talk over our concerns, and check in with our intentions, both people will know there's a problem or a possibility of parting. If we stay in an adult state, we won't try to persuade someone to stay against his or her will. We wouldn't want to be with someone who doesn't genuinely want to be with us.

The key is to remember that people hurt others because they are unconscious or unaware. *If only we could, even for just a fleeting moment, grasp that we would all love each other if we could,* if we were free from the armor we have used to shield our hearts. When we realize that the enemy is unconsciousness, not another person, we will bring fresh air to our bitterness, and create more spaciousness in our minds and hearts.

So while there are at least fifty ways to leave a lover, there is only one kind of compassion. When you show kindness and understanding to another, it will touch that soft spot in your heart and theirs, and set you both free.

41

Stair Steps to Heaven:
get in, get out, move on, and learn

Everything in our lives can wake us up or put us to sleep,
and basically it's up to us to let it wake us up.
— PEMA CHODRON

Some people learn and grow through one primary
relationship that lasts a lifetime. Others learn through a
series of relationships. There is no right or wrong way.
Growth comes from recognizing our patterns, being
willing to explore them, and not repeating the story
lines that keep us stuck.

Sonia came from an emotionally withholding family
and internalized a belief that she didn't deserve love. By
age thirty-eight, she'd been in several painful relationships with people who were cold and emotionally
withholding. 'I had five relationships, but it might as well
have been one, they were so much the same,' Sonia
lamented.

Only when she joined a therapy group, committed
herself to her own growth, defined a bottom line and

stuck to it, was she able to break her negative pattern. I've observed many people over the years who eventually found good relationships, in spite of a painful history of abuse or harmful relationships. They were willing to get involved with someone, observe themselves, learn whatever lessons were presented, and move on if there wasn't a good fit. They didn't hang onto mediocre relationships and they were willing to spend periods of time being alone.

One client described it as walking up a staircase. 'You meet someone, stick to your bottom line, learn from it and, if it doesn't work, you take another step up.' These people were willing to self-confront and meet the mud and the goblins that blocked them from love. They'd walk right into their own fears, walls, and blocks and were willing to feel the anxiety, pain, and grief that had created armor around their hearts. They asked for support to bring up concerns, to trust themselves and listen to their doubts. This process sometimes took a few years or several relationships, but eventually, most of them were successful.

The people who got stuck tried to make a poor match work, ignored their observations, and were guided by stories such as 'I've got to make this work. There might never be anyone else.' They might see troublesome behavior on the first few dates, but instead of confronting it, they'd still be complaining about it six months later. Or they'd deceive themselves. *I don't mind if he's always late, drunk, sad, inconsiderate, and preoccupied. I'm not angry, hurt, or frustrated. It's all right if she never makes love to me or cares about what I want.* Then they'd deceive themselves about their deception

228

and convince themselves they were being patient and caring.

Some of the often told stories we use to con ourselves:

1. It's getting better.
2. Nobody's perfect.
3. S/he had a hard childhood.
4. I know s/he really loves me, s/he just has a hard time showing it.
5. S/he has so much potential. I'm sure it will get better.

Don't ever marry potential or plan on someone changing. Ask yourself, why would it get better? Why would this person change? Behavior patterns are hard-wired into the limbic system of the brain and are reinforced through thousands or millions of repetitions. It takes a powerful commitment and deep inner work to release old patterns, and it takes time.

Creating a healthy relationship often means confronting ourselves, not the other person. Mark, a client, told me, 'I have to confront Vera. She's never on time, she interrupts me, she flirts with other men, and she's hurt if I don't want to be sexual. I've brought these things up repeatedly and nothing has changed.'

Mark didn't need to confront Vera. He needed to confront himself. Why was he staying with a person who has so many traits that bother him? There comes a time amidst all the discussion, therapy, and processing to say, *That's the way she is. Do I want to be with her as she is today? Not tomorrow, not when her potential is realized, not in five years. Is there enough glue to have a relationship right now, and can I live with the rest?*

If Mark had set a bottom line and stuck to it, he would have stopped seeing Vera after three dates. He would have brought up his concerns once or twice, and when nothing changed, he would have kindly said good-bye. If we stay in a relationship when we know there isn't a fit, it becomes *our* problem. We need to continually ask ourselves, *What do I need to learn?* Usually it's something profound, such as 'you can't get blood out of a stone' – a tough lesson for many of us.

Sufis talk about attunement. As you attune to a higher vibration of energy through becoming clear and open, you will more quickly see when there is potential for a good relationship. You will also be attracted to others who are growing and stretching and more likely to be a worthy companion for you on the journey.

42

Notice the Bittersweet Moments of New Love

We've been seeing each other for several months. We feel a durable fire growing between us as our relationship becomes more anchored in experience and trust. We've made it through an argument, we've cried, we've felt delight in each other's company and come to laugh more easily. He enjoys the same music at the same volume, she follows through on phone calls and plans, there's an easy rhythm and flow in deciding on a movie, or spending a leisurely Saturday together, we suddenly realize it's one in the morning and we've been talking in the hot tub for two hours. You like her friends, he shows up with a tiger lily in a blue vase. So why do we sometimes feel a sudden letdown when we realize this is the person we've been waiting for?

All decisions, all steps forward, involve loss. I first felt this sudden pang of melancholy at the age of thirty when I got my dream job as a piano instructor at Ohio University in Athens, Ohio. My goal since the age of seven had been to be a college instructor of piano.

When I received the phone call from the head of the Ohio University music department at 2 p.m. offering me the job, I was elated. By 7:00 that evening I was feeling blue. I was puzzled. That night at a party, a psychologist friend explained it to me. There is a psychological moment when a dream comes to fruition, and we must shut off all other possibilities. If I decide to be with this one and only person, I am also saying, 'There is no one else I will ever be with. No more scanning the horizon for possibilities, no more dreaming or fantasies.'

I recalled that piano job experience years later when I woke up feeling a dusky melancholy the morning after spending a wonderful day with a new love. I realized it was this person – perfect, imperfect, with strengths and weaknesses – who I wanted to be with. As I lay there, feeling a heaviness in my heart, my ego mind flashed on comparisons to past relationships: 'He isn't as adoring as Noel. He doesn't have much financial security.' I wondered if I was sensing a deeper knowing that he wasn't the right person for me, or if it was my fear speaking – the fear of letting go of all other possibilities and accepting this perfectly imperfect human being into my life.

Every time we open one door, we close another. It's lovely to spend Sunday morning with our new love, cooking breakfast and taking a walk together. But in the midst of our happiness, we may feel nostalgia for our former Sunday morning ritual of uninterrupted time alone at a favorite restaurant reading the newspaper. We need to acknowledge the presence of both excitement and loss, to feel their rhythm as they ebb and flow through a new relationship. If we try to deny our losses, they lead to resentments, a gnawing discomfort, and a desire to withdraw.

Yet we also need to remind our ego that love means letting go of our entrenched rituals, of comparing, of wanting life to stay the same. Some people crawl out of their shell for a little while to taste a new relationship, but because their ego is attached to security, predictability, and former rituals, they decide to retreat. Entering a relationship and living in the heart of the Beloved means our life will change, our shells will crack open and we will never be the same again.

43

Help the Relationship Expand with Creativity and Playfulness

Nothing stands still. Whatever doesn't grow withers and dies.

If we aren't growing, we're going backward. To keep a relationship alive means exploring our capacity *as a couple* to have fun, try new ventures, and create a special language of the relationship. Each person can help expand a relationship by initiating new experiences and making clear requests to find out if their new love will join them in their heartfelt desires.

In getting to know Andrew, the man I met when I finished my first book, I wanted to know if he would take an interest in my writing because it was such an important part of my life. Although he had casually asked about my book, and I had vaguely mentioned that I'd like him to read some of it, nothing happened. So instead of waiting for him to ask, I called him and said, 'I'd love your feedback on something I'm writing. Can

I send you a chapter right now?' He said yes. (Of course I sent him the chapter on sex!)

To make it even easier for him to respond, I included a list of questions: 'Please tell me what parts you like, what doesn't have flow, what is missing,' and so on. By doing this I opened the field to finding out if he could join me in my personal world, something I yearned for. To my delight, he read the chapter, gave me some helpful feedback, and we ended up having a heartfelt conversation about sexuality.

If you want something to happen, help it happen. Don't complain that you never cook together, watch a particular video, or go dancing. Take action, initiate. People who get results are usually excellent at making specific requests bolstered by self-confidence. They enjoy stretching their limits and experimenting. They also believe they deserve what they are asking for. People who don't get what they want often complain, make muffled pleas or vague suggestions, then feel mad that their wishes aren't fulfilled.

Remember, it's crucial to make a specific request and suggest a time: 'I'd like to cook dinner together next Friday evening.' 'I'd like to practice dancing before we go out this Saturday so I won't feel self-conscious on the dance floor.' 'I'd like us to read love poems to each other in bed. [Have a book ready.]' 'I'd like to plan a camping trip for next weekend.'

By doing this, you get a clearer picture of the potential of the relationship. If she says, 'I don't want to read poems in bed, I think it's silly,' then you know that if you choose this person, reading poems in bed is something you will live without. If he says, 'I hate camping' when

235

you suggest an outdoor adventure, then accept that you will camp alone or with other people forever. By making requests and seeing if the other person is receptive, you find out where you meet and where you don't. You will know the positive aspects and limitations of being with this person so you can make an informed choice.

A variation on this theme is to simply take action. Bring a book of love poems to bed, touch your lover tenderly and when the time feels right, read one. See how she reacts. When I was becoming involved with Jessie, who seemed very practical, I figured she would think I was corny to set a pretty dinner table with flowers, candles, and the good silverware. But because I love to create a beautiful atmosphere, I did it anyhow. Much to my delight, Jessie smiled, touched the flowers and said warmly, 'This is so lovely. My family never did anything like this.' I also read the ecstatic poems of Kabir to her while snuggled up in our little tent on a camping trip.

When you become proactive, playful, and assertive, you bring a sparkling energy to the relationship and become a catalyst for both of you to break new ground.

One caveat with this approach: both people must be honest and not fake pleasure or enjoyment. Often, people don't try something new because no one ever showed them how, or they are blocked by inertia, so being introduced to something new is a blessing. Other times, after a few tries, a person just isn't interested. Someone might accompany you doing something on occasion to please you, but he or she needs to be honest and admit it's not really something he or she would choose if you weren't around.

Likewise, we need to be slow in refusing a request unless it feels like an inner violation to our values. Remember, your new love is opening their heart, asking you to join in their pleasure. If you are always saying no, you are shutting the door of connection.

If you're not sure you want to take part in some activity, express your doubts but don't slam the door. You might have a nice surprise.

Andrew arrived for our first date at an outdoor cafe riding a motorcycle. A motorcycle! My stereotype of men on motorcycles was a bunch of testosterone announcing itself to the world by gunning the engine and showing off. Fortunately, I was totally charmed by Andrew and, while I didn't accept his invitation for a ride that day, I didn't close the door either.

A few weeks later, when he invited me to join him on a ride to a waterfall up in the mountains where we could take a hike, I could hear how much it meant to him. As we started up the road, a big laugh exploded inside me. *Here I am, nearly fifty, on the back of a motorcycle! Where else will life take me?* As my mind quieted down, I started to feel the breeze on my face. Then slowly, as I relaxed, I began to appreciate the unfettered view of the pine trees, the balsam root, and a wide array of spring wildflowers. I can't say I'll ever be a motorcycle enthusiast, but I did agree to another ride, and, more important, I felt pleasure by joining him in something he loved.

So remember, you might feel awkward or silly trying something new, but you might also have a good laugh, open up your heart, move beyond your prejudices and end up dancing closer to your beloved.

Part 6

LIVING IN THE HEART OF THE BELOVED:
we are one with each other

44

Enjoy the Special Story of How You Met

If you watch couples ballroom dancing, you'll notice that while there's only one song being played, every couple has a different flow, quality, and rhythm. The same is true for the process of creating a relationship. There are no pat phrases or skills that guarantee romance or an enduring relationship.

Every couple creates a unique story as they come together. One of the greatest joys in writing this book was asking couples how they met. The tender glances, laughter, quibbling over details, and recounting that special time in their lives reflected their special journey. What is your story so far?

When I recently asked Shahir, my Sufi teacher and her husband, Sadiq, what kindled their romance, they both laughed heartily. Sadiq and Shahir had known each other for a long time as active members of the Peace Dance community – both as leaders and participants. 'I thought she was an outrageous and not very intelligent woman,' Sadiq said.

'I couldn't stand him at first,' Shahir said, laughing. 'I thought he was a conceited man who got off on having lots of women chase after him.'

The bridge was crossed when Shahir had a near-fatal stroke and asked him to come visit her, not knowing he was a Reiki healing master. When he arrived, although she could barely talk, she was able to get out the words 'I want some of your heat, your fire.'

'I needed healing and he needed someone to help him develop his healing talents, so we were a good fit. I couldn't talk because that part of my brain didn't work, so I could only accept what he gave, which was very freeing for both of us.'

Within six weeks they were lovers. 'That was what I really wanted,' Shahir said. 'Sex. I was twenty-eight thousand miles away from my body, and I wanted the aliveness and connection of sex and intimacy to help me get back inside myself. I realized, from having nearly died, that when you're alive, that's what you're supposed to be doing, being alive. There's plenty of time to be dead.' Again she laughed. Shahir and Sadiq's relationship flowered into a deeply felt connection between them.

Maggie, a warm-spirited woman, moved to Wyoming where she was told to look up Ed, the friend of a friend. She called Ed and asked if she could join 'his gang' to go to the movies one Friday night. He said 'sure.' She initiated contact several more times and felt an attraction growing before he finally reciprocated. Once he started to show interest, Maggie held herself back to see if he would come forward. Within four months they moved in together and they have since built a house and set a wedding date. It never would have happened if Maggie hadn't initiated the first, second, and third times together. When she later asked him why it took him so long to reach out to her, he said he couldn't imagine such a wonderful woman would want him.

I was amazed at how often people knew at first sight that they had met the person they wanted to marry. This was confirmed by Barry Sinrod's and Marlo Grey's book *Just Married*, which presents fascinating data on newly married couples. Eighty-six percent of men and forty-one percent of women they interviewed said it had been love at first sight. It brought to mind a conversation I'd had with Margie and Stan, a vibrant, attractive couple I met at a nearby health club. I was sitting beside Margie on an exercise bike when she told me their story, which dated back forty-eight years.

'I was a freshman in college and a girlfriend came to me and said, "There's a guy who wants to take you out." "No blind dates," I told her in no uncertain terms. "I don't go out with people I don't know." The friend persisted, saying, "He's really nice, and so eager to meet you." "No. I'm not interested," I insisted. After a couple months, and numerous requests, I finally said, "Okay, I'll meet him." The date was pleasant, but I wasn't particularly interested.'

'So what happened?' I asked.

She grinned. 'He was persistent. So I kept going out with him.'

'Was there a time you fell in love?' I asked.

'No, it just got better and better and, gradually, I knew I wanted to be with him.'

'Where did he first see you?' I asked.

She laughed again. 'He saw me leaving an English class and told his friend, "I just saw the woman I'm going to marry." '

Whether you initiated the first date, were sought out, used an ad, met on a blind date, met him or her while walking your dog, or suddenly had a cosmic connection with an old friend, your story of meeting your special person is unique and special. Don't try to fit yourself into a mold. Let the story write you.

45

Little Commitments:
the daily bread of intimacy

From cane reeds, sugar.
From a worm's cocoon, silk.

Be patient if you can, and from sour
grapes will come something sweet.
—RUMI, from *Say I Am You*

True commitment comes from the heart and cannot be forced. It's not so much that we 'make' a commitment as that we are led by a desire to deepen the bond between us. Commitments provide a protective boundary around a couple so they can bring up conflict, explore sexuality, ask questions, and reveal their inner world. Without some form of agreement to stay together, even if it's for four months or a year, people tend to protect themselves by holding back. It's a biological survival mechanism.

Little commitments can vary widely in scope. We might commit to stop seeing other people, be monogamous, and not withdraw when there are differences to be talked over. We agree to spend weekends together, to join in experiencing each other's favorite pastimes. Commitments are a way to define a relationship.

I've had fledging couples come for counseling who had no definition of their relationship. I'd ask, 'Are you being sexual?' They'd nod. Had they agreed on being monogamous? They'd look at each other quizzically. 'Well, I assume so,' one would say. The other person would hedge: 'Well, mostly.' When I asked them to describe their level of commitment, I'd often get highly contradictory responses or comments like 'We just want to keep it spontaneous.'

People usually maintain nebulous boundaries out of fear: fear that if you ask for commitment the other person will refuse; fear that if you make a commitment, you'll break it; or fear that you'll be swallowed up and lose yourself. The ability to commit is related to levels of differentiation. Because people who are well differentiated are better able to hang onto themselves in close relationship to others, commitment feels like freedom to go deeper, feel union, and explore oneself.

A commitment to another person is always a commitment to know ourselves and do whatever it takes to fulfill our agreements. If we promise to be truthful, we commit to a deep level of inner awareness and to confronting any fear that blocks us from being truthful.

Another aspect of commitment is making the relationship known to close friends and family. By telling others of the relationship, it becomes more real to ourselves. It also allows the new couple to be included *as a couple* in social gatherings. If your partner doesn't want friends and family to know about your relationship, or doesn't want to socialize with others *as a couple*, or you feel like a well-kept secret, you are probably with someone who will be unable to commit to a spiritually centered relationship.

The cousin of commitment is keeping agreements. *Keeping agreements is a sign of a person who knows who he or she is.* A conscious person can know she would like to have lunch and see a movie next Saturday, and can clear the way to do so. Making agreements also provides a measure for testing our ability to follow through on what we say we will do.

People who continually break agreements, and then provide a litany of excuses, are poor candidates for a relationship, no matter what flowery declarations of love they whisper in your ear. Likewise, if you continue to date someone who breaks agreements, you need to confront yourself: *Why am I staying with someone who is so unreliable? If s/he can't do something as simple as keeping a Friday night date, what does the future hold?*

In a balanced relationship, both people will be active in defining the level of commitment. Equivocating about commitment may signal ambivalence about this particular relationship, or a problem committing to anyone. While you can't force commitments – they must come from the heart – they are a prerequisite for moving forward and creating intimacy. Without them you are likely to stay in limbo and never deepen your connection. It's often tempting to talk ourselves out of what we see, but if we stay with someone who isn't committed to the relationship, we slide into illusions and tumble off our path into the mud. Relationships are meant to be a celebration of love, creativity, joy, and growth, not an endless experience of pain, unhappiness, and loneliness. Life hands us enough hard lessons free of charge.

Sometimes people push for commitments out of desperation. They want to jump over the uneasy process of getting to know each other and say 'we're partners' or 'we're engaged' because it brings an illusory sense of security.

When someone pushes for commitment too soon, it can reflect insecurity and desperation rather than love. Remember, you can't force a commitment. It must come from a desire to go deeper into a relationship. If a commitment doesn't come from such a desire, it's pretense.

The process of commitment can elicit a mixture of delight and fear. One moment you are thrilled at the thought of a long-term relationship, the next minute you go blank with fear. *Oh my God, this is for real.* When you feel yourself getting squeezed this way, you need to breathe into your fear. Stay with yourself – explore your fears, and practice Tonglin. Ask yourself, *Is my fear grounded in reality? Is there something wrong here, or am I bumping into a frightened heart that created the story, 'it's dangerous to love, to get close, to let anyone really love me'?* If the fear persists, see if you can free yourself of whatever is in the way so you can clear your vision and make wise choices.

As you commit to each other, keep agreements, and find delight in being together, you go beyond the flight of wild romance and begin to feast on the daily bread of a steadfast bond.

46

Taking Stock:
listening to your Buddha nature

True commitment is born of knowledge. We can't say yes to what we don't know. As you spend more and more time with your new love, it's natural to start contemplating a major commitment. As you move in this direction, it is important to 'take stock' of your relationship, to be mindful of it. I have included some thoughts to help you explore all your feelings so you can make the best possible decision.

Make some quiet time for yourself. Think through everything about your partner – your doubts, your fears, and your joys. Write them all down, then sit quietly and hear what else comes up. Keep writing until you feel completely cleared out of all your thoughts and your mind becomes still.

Another approach is to rate yourself 1 (low) – 10 (high) on the following items for your partner. Write down whatever number first pops into your head and let yourself be surprised. Be honest. If you want to write down a high and low score to show the extremes, that can be interesting as well.

PARTNER / SELF

_____/_____ Fun to be with.

_____/_____ Initiates being together.

_____/_____ Committed to monogamy/able to be monogamous (if that is what you want).

_____/_____ Committed to his or her own spiritual journey – able to reflect, have insight into his or her own behavior, be honest.

_____/_____ Reliability/responsibility – is on time, keeps agreements.

_____/_____ Enjoys pursuing common interests and activities together.

_____/_____ Is sincerely interested in what matters to you – asks questions, responds.

_____/_____ Sexual attraction level.

_____/_____ Is present and responsive during lovemaking, if applicable (highest and lowest score).

_____/_____ Able to discuss conflicts and work together solving problems.

_____/_____ Demonstrates ability to confront him- or herself.

_____/_____ Apologizes when late or does something inconsiderate.

_____/_____ Your overall feelings and attraction for this person.

_____/_____ Your overall prediction of success of this relationship.

You should also write down your other concerns, pleasures, and thoughts – everything that comes to mind.

This is the picture of your prospective partner. Did numbers pop into your head that were much higher or lower than you wanted? Did you find yourself wanting to fudge on your responses? How does it *feel* when you look it over? Don't analyze or rationalize. Just let yourself feel. Don't make a phone call, drink coffee, or wash the dishes. Just sit and take stock.

Now, use the above list to rate *yourself*. How does the picture look when you put the two scores side by side? It can be fascinating if both of you do the ratings and compare them.

If you are contemplating a commitment to someone as a life partner or spouse, accept in every cell of your body that you take this person exactly as they are at this moment. You agree to the whole package deal just the way it is. For example, if someone is not good at expressing feelings, accept that trait now and forever. Promise yourself you won't harp on it. If your partner needs a lot of time alone, accept that need and expect the pattern to continue. In fact, expect everything to continue just as it is. Will that be okay with you in six months? A year? Five years? It might seem like a contradiction to base a current decision only on the present moment, when impermanence is one of the basics of Buddhism. The point is this: *To make a decision based on reality, we have to accept that it will be this way forever because the present time is the only truth we have.* Otherwise, our decision is based on projections and wishful thinking.

The rating scale may be very high and reassuring, or it may raise some serious doubts for you and your partner. If you are uneasy, talk frankly with your partner about your concerns, wait a few weeks and do the rating again. You may try seeing a counselor to sort out the differences or trouble spots. It may get better, it may decline. Take refuge in the Buddha by remembering that your joy and peace of mind are tied to being true to yourself by walking a path of kindness and compassion. Then put away the lists, sit back, breathe, and listen with a finely tuned ear to that still quiet place of wisdom that is your Buddha nature.

47

Big Commitments:
the samaya 'marriage'

Vows commit us to the work ahead, psychological and spiritual. They insist we cultivate mercy and awareness. That we do the work it takes to offer all we are.
　　　　　　　　　　　—STEPHEN AND ONDREA LEVINE,
　　　　　　　　　　　　　　　Embracing the Beloved

Our commitment to a lover is embodied in our commitment to the spiritual path. We make a vow to do whatever it takes to be present in the relationship, which is the same as making a vow to be present to ourselves. Pema Chodron describes *samaya*, a Buddhist term, as 'a marriage to reality.'

In the case of samaya, when we talk about commitment, it's total commitment: total commitment to sanity, total commitment to our experience, an unconditional relationship with reality. Our deepest commitment is our commitment to reality . . . In relationships, the challenges are to give in, to surrender our way to doing things, and

not to split when we feel threatened. Basically the
challenge is to be genuine – to feel our pounding heart or
shaking knees or whatever it is, and stick with it. In a
nutshell, very few of us ever allow ourselves to be in
a situation that doesn't have at least a teensy-weensy little
exit, a place where we can get out if we have to.

—PEMA CHODRON

The more you close all the escape hatches and open your eyes and heart to your beloved, the greater the possibility for an enduring, abiding union. As you commit to reality, to staying conscious, you will experience the joy of becoming more alive and present to yourself and your Beloved.

What a blessing when two people can say to each other, unequivocally, 'You are the person I want as my lover, my special one, my partner on the journey, my Beloved. I will devote myself to you, to us. I will close the doors on all others. I accept you with all your imperfections. I accept you with all your beauty, wonder, and strength.'

What would it be like to say, 'I'm here, I'm going to stay present and not run when things get tough?' What would it be like to let go of the little rituals and hiding places we use as escape hatches, and dive in wholeheartedly? What would it be like to open our heart completely, to not indulge in the security of holding back, hiding, keeping secrets?

Samaya means not holding anything back, not preparing
our escape route, not looking for alternatives, not thinking

that there is ample time to do things later . . . It softens us
so that we can't deceive ourselves.

—PEMA CHODRON

In a committed relationship we walk *toward* our fears, we breathe them in, we practice Tonglin. We open up. Through unconditional honesty with this one person, we come to have an unconditional honesty with the world, with all people, or, as Sufis might say, through loving each other wholeheartedly, your love expands to embrace all people. When we live in current reality we develop a heightened state of awareness to taste, smells, sounds, colors, beauty, and touch. We enjoy the sensuousness of caressing velvet, of stroking our beloved's hair, of looking at a single rose, of smelling garlic cooking, of listening to our partner's breathing as she falls asleep. We are tuned into the moment. Resonant. Alive.

Making a long-term commitment is something to consecrate and celebrate. You might want to create a ritual, have a small gathering of friends, take a weekend trip, announce that you are engaged, exchange rings – whatever connects for you. But most of all, savor the feeling in your heart. You have walked the path and now you have been given a gift of someone to journey beside you.

48

When Nothing Works:
remember lovers are a gift from the universe

For everything there is a season,
And a time for every purpose under heaven
— ECCLESIASTES 3:1

Sometimes we open our heart, date lots of people, and stay true to our path, yet no lover is forthcoming. This tests our faith and our ability to accept what we are given. If you feel discouraged, you can remember there is a mystery to life beyond our comprehension. Ultimately, lovers are a gift from the universe. There may be absolutely nothing wrong – no deep block, no problem, nothing you could have done differently. It's just not your time right now, for no particular reason. Your path is to find acceptance, to be at peace with yourself.

People have different views on why we do or don't find a partner: some believe it's related to karma or to God's will, while others believe it is simply a random event. Whatever you believe, the truth is that we are not in complete control. The more we accept this, the more we will be at peace.

Perhaps this is your time to journey on your own. Perhaps it is your time to take on a project, return to school, or learn a new skill with the freedom and clear focus that's possible when one is single. But whatever the reason a lover has not appeared, you need not be alone. You are the lover in your life. You are a child of the universe, a child of Spirit.

Remember the words of St Francis of Assisi: 'Make me an instrument of thy peace.' The happiest people I know – whether single or with a partner – are dedicated to helping relieve suffering in the world. They help grow gardens, visit the sick, contribute to community projects and radiate a bright spirit.

Ultimately, life is about knowing who we are and being able to accept the inexplicable rhythm and pulse of our journeys. We move from asking *Why me?* to reflecting on what befalls us. We learn to say, *This is my life right now. What can I make of it? What can I learn from it? How can I feel joy?* We are all made of the same substance, we are all part of the same cosmic essence, of all that is. It is only our illusions that keep us feeling separate and alone.

When my Sufi teacher, Shahir, suffered her near-fatal stroke, she experienced leaving her body and moving into the light before saying, 'I've got to come back. I have four children.' She spoke about it.

In the stroke, I went to that place of the void. There I was in the void looking at a point of light out there and a point of light in here, and I realized it was my soul, and that there was no duality, no separation of anything. There is no 'in here' and 'out there' because everything is one. We are the light and we are the dark, which is the point of surrender. I discovered that we're always in love, we're bathed in it.

49

Tasting the Sweetness:
remember you are love, lover, and beloved

If you have the blessing of finding your beloved, look her softly in the eyes, touch him tenderly, see into the heart of this special being who wants the same things as you do – to be understood, loved, and respected, to find purpose and to find themselves.

You have a primary partner, a shelter from the storm, a companion, helpmate, lover, and friend. You also have a sparring partner who will help you learn more about conflict, tolerance, compassion, and forgiveness. You will meet more and more parts of you that are all part of your Buddha nature. Welcome whatever comes with your heart, the same way you meet your beloved – openly, honestly, fearlessly.

The vitality and joy of your relationship will reflect the vitality and joy of each of you as you continue to awaken. By honoring your commitments, loving each other well, and staying firmly planted in current reality, you open yourselves to a transcendent love that is between you and all around you. To know one person well is to know everything well – to become one with love, with all lovers, and with the Beloved. Over time you will attune even more deeply to each other, creating a harmony all your own, a language of your special connection. There is great richness when the river of spirit flows between two open hearts, allowing them to give and receive, to join together in the mystical heart of the Beloved.

Recently, I took part in the Sufi wedding of Shahir and Sadiq, whom I mentioned earlier. 'We decided to get married because we knew we wanted to live in the third body that is created in union with each other,' Shahir told me.

Their marriage was an integral part of a Sufi weekend retreat entitled 'How Do We Celebrate?', held at a church camp by Lake Coeur d'Alene in Idaho. It was an annual gathering that included a close-knit core of people on the Sufi path and others who shared a love for the Dances of Universal Peace and enjoyed weekend retreats.

The only prior planning for the wedding was scheduling Saturday morning for the ceremony. Otherwise, there were no invitations and no formal arrangements. Whoever was at the weekend gathering was automatically invited. Preparation for the wedding took less than two hours. Women picked branches, shrubbery, and flowers and combined them with huge silk scarves to transform the corner of the large dining hall into an arboretum of wonder and delight.

The ceremony started outside. The men formed one group, the women another, bedecked with scarves, chiffon, and garlands of flowers. Both groups carried drums. The two groups in procession approached each other, the men coming out of the woods across a field, ambling slowly to the beat of the drums, meeting the women who came from near the lake – radiant, joyful, all of us rich in spirit from two days of dancing and doing Sufi practices. As the two groups met, the drumbeats joined in a single rhythm.

Shahir and Sadiq joined arms and entered the marriage room under an archway of hands, singing, '*Gunga ki Jai Jai*,' which signifies the two rivers that join together to become the Ganges. All of us did a serpentine dance, arm in arm, winding in and out making archways for everyone to pass through. Eventually, Shahir and Sadiq sat down facing each other in front of the 'altar,' a table covered by a gold cloth, adorned by nine candles, eight of them symbolizing a major spiritual tradition of the world – including the Christian, Jewish, Buddhist, Hindu, Muslim, Zoroastrian, indigenous, and goddess approaches to spirituality. One by one, each candle was lit and a member of the wedding party read from scriptures of that spiritual tradition. This was followed by a peace dance performed by everyone in a circle around the bride and groom, who remained seated, facing each other.

What a wonderful thing, I thought to myself, *to be married in unity with the deepest wisdom of all religions, to invoke a blessing on all people, and not make separation from anyone.* Finally, after all the candles were lit, the Sufi teacher, called a Murshida, led the marriage ceremony. At one point she asked Sadiq and Shahir if they had any vows.

Sadiq said, 'I will do my very best to keep my heart open to you through anger, doubt, and fear.'

Shahir leaned forward toward Sadiq, her face radiant. 'I have no vow,' she said, 'All I want to say is, I am happy to meet your company.'

As I drove home afterward, I mused about the many types of wedding ceremonies throughout the world, both known and unknown to me. What seemed special about Shahir and Sadiq's wedding was that it symbolized in many ways the essence of the spiritual path – love, kindness, being in the moment, and speaking spontaneously from the heart. Even the scriptures that were read from the various religious traditions were the choice of the reader. The spontaneity would have challenged the ego of anyone needing a tight formula or control.

There are hundreds of ways to sanctify and bless your relationship, to join together as one with love, lover, and beloved. Find your way. Let it express all of who you are. The more your union reflects your luminous spirit, the more you bring light and joy to each other, the more you will feel yourselves as one with the Beloved. Your union can be a beacon for others as you bring devotion, truth, humor, and compassion to each other.

If, for just a moment, whenever you see the Beloved, which is in all people, you pause, breathe and say *namaste* 'I honor that of God in you,' or 'I bow to the light in you' you will have a touchstone to remind you of the shining jewel within both of you.

Namaste,
Your Sister,
Charlotte Sophia

Recommended Reading

Instead of providing an extensive bibliography, I have listed some of my favorite authors of books on dating, relationships, and spirituality.

Dating

DeAngelis, Barbara, Ph.D. *Are You the One for Me?*
Page, Susan. *If I'm So Wonderful, Why Am I Still Single?*
Sinrod, Barry, and Marlo Grey. *Just Married.*

Relationships

Buber, Martin. *I and Thou.*
Chopra, Deepak. *The Path to Love: Renewing the Power of Spirit in Your Life.*
Fromm, Erich. *The Art of Loving.*
Johnson, Catherine. *Lucky in Love.*
Kasl, Charlotte Davis, Ph.D. *Women, Sex, and Addiction: A Search for Love and Power.*
———. *A Home for the Heart: Creating Intimacy and Community with Loved Ones, Neighbors, and Friends.*

——. *Finding Joy: 101 Ways to Free Your Spirit and Dance with Life.*

Levine, Stephen, and Ondrea Levine. *Embracing the Beloved: Relationship as a Path of Awakening.*

Pearsall, Paul. *Sexual Healing: Using the Power of an Intimate, Loving Relationship to Heal Your Body and Soul.*

Scarf, Maggie. *Intimate Partners: Patterns in Love and Marriage.*

Buddhism and related topics

Beck, Charlotte Joko. *Everyday Zen: Love and Work; Nothing Special: Living Zen.*

Boorstein, Sylvia. *It's Easier Than You Think* and other titles.

Chodron, Pema. *Start Where You Are: A Guide to Compassionate Living.*

——. *When Things Fall Apart: Heart Advice for Difficult Times.*

——. *The Wisdom of No Escape and the Path of Loving-Kindness.*

Dalai Lama, His Holiness. *The World of Tibetan Buddhism: An Overview of Its Philosophy and Practice.*

Das, Lama Surya. *Awakening the Buddha Within.*

Hanh, Thich Nhat. *Peace Is Every Step: The Path of Mindfulness in Everyday Life.*

Spirituality

Dass, Ram. *Journey of Awakening: A Meditator's Guidebook* and many others.

Gibran, Kahlil. *The Prophet.*

Khan, Hazrat Inayat. *The Complete Sayings.*

Krishnamurti, J. *The Book of Life.*

Matt, Daniel C. *The Essential Kabbalah: The Heart of Jewish Mysticism.*

Shaw, Miranda. *Passionate Enlightenment: Women in Tantric Buddhism.*

Welwood, John, Ph.D. *Journey of the Heart: The Path of Conscious Love.*

Poetry

Barks, Coleman, translator, et al. *Say I Am You: Poetry Interspersed with Stories of Rumi and Shams.*

Barks, Coleman, and John Moyne, translators. *The Essential Rumi, Like That, Say I Am You,* and others.

Bly, Robert. *The Kabir Book: Forty-four of the Ecstatic Poems of Kabir.*

Psychology

Miller, Jean Baker, M.D. *Toward a New Psychology of Women.*

Wolinsky, Stephen. *The Tao of Chaos: Essence and the Enneagram.*

——. *Quantum Consciousness: The Guide to Experiencing Quantum Psychology.*

——. *Trances People Live: Healing Approaches in Quantum Psychology.*

——. *The Dark Side of the Inner Child: The Next Step.*

Resources

Handwriting Analysis

Jane Yank, M.A., Signature Consulting, (651) 776-7599
email: janeyank@bitstream.net

Intensive Psychotherapy

I (Charlotte Kasl) am available for intensive psychotherapy sessions for individuals and couples (8–16 hours). I
use a combination of EMDR, ego state therapy, hypnosis,
quantum psychology, and body movement. I also draw on
research and teachings of John Gottman for couples therapy.
I am a Licensed Clinical Counselor in Montana, formerly
a Licensed Psychologist in Minnesota (1983–1998), and a
Certified Addiction Specialist. Call (406) 273-6080 for
information.

EMDR (Eye Movement Desensitization and Reprocessing)

This is an advanced technology for releasing traumatic
memories, changing negative core beliefs and behavior

patterns, and overcoming addictive and compulsive behavior. It is very focused, efficient, and effective. For more information you can read *EMDR* by Francine Shapiro, published by HarperCollins. For a therapist in your area, or for information, write or call EMDR, P.O. Box 51010, Pacific Grove, CA 93950, phone: (831) 372-3900, fax: (831) 647-9881

Correspondence

I love to receive letters and read them all, but I can't promise to respond. I am available for workshops, talks, consulting, and therapist trainings on a variety of topics related to dating, relationships, overcoming addiction with the 16-step empowerment model, finding joy, and personal empowerment. For more information on my other books, order forms, information on the 16 steps for empowerment, or a list of workshops, see my web site at www.charlottekasl.com

If you want a list of workshops and don't have access to the internet, send a self addressed, stamped envelope to

Charlotte Kasl
P.O. Box 1302
Lolo, MT 59847
Phone: (406) 273-6080, fax: (406) 273-0111

Charlotte Kasl, Ph.D., formerly a professional piano instructor, has been a practising psychotherapist, workshop leader, Quaker, and Reiki healer for over twenty years. She has had a longtime involvement with feminism, Eastern spiritual practices, and alternative healing, bringing an empowering holistic approach to all her work. Her books include *Finding Joy*, *Many Roads, One Journey*, and the classic *Women, Sex, and Addiction: A Search for Love and Power*. Formerly of Minneapolis, Minnesota, she now lives in an octagonal house on a mountain near Missoula, Montana.

A SELECTION OF NON-FICTION TITLES
AVAILABLE FROM BANTAM BOOKS